CHRISTMAS
JOYS

Books by Joan Winmill Brown

CHRISTMAS JOYS
NO LONGER ALONE
WINGS OF JOY
EVERY KNEE SHALL BOW
CORRIE: THE LIVES SHE'S TOUCHED
TOGETHER EACH DAY

CHRISTMAS JOYS

Compiled and Edited by
JOAN WINMILL BROWN

Illustrations by Lynn Stephens Lieppman

A Doubleday-Galilee Original/Doubleday & Company, Inc.
Garden City, New York
1982

Grateful acknowledgment is made to the following for permission to reprint their copyrighted material.

Every reasonable effort has been made to trace the ownership of all copyrighted material included in this volume. Any errors which may have occurred are inadvertent and will be corrected in subsequent editions, provided notification is sent to the publisher.

"A Christmas Smile" by Gil Beers. As it appeared in *Moody Monthly*. Reprinted by permission of the author.

"The Manger's Message" by the Reverend Dr. B. Clayton Bell, M.Div.; D.D. Reprinted by permission of the author.

"How Far to Bethlehem?" by Sylvia Dooling. Reprinted by permission of the author.

Excerpt from "What Shall We Do This Christmas?" by Colleen Townsend Evans. Reprinted by permission of the author.

Excerpt from "I Know—I've Been There" by Louis H. Evans, Jr., Pastor, National Presbyterian Church, Washington, D.C. Reprinted by permission of the author.

Excerpt from "A Day of Pleasant Bread" from *Adventures in Friendship* by David Grayson. Copyright 1910 by Doubleday & Company, Inc. Copyright 1908, 1909, 1910 by The Phillips Publishing Company. Reprinted by permission of Mrs. John A. MacDonald.

"Receive the Gift" by Richard C. Halverson, Chaplain, U. S. Senate. Reprinted by permission of the author.

"The Living Word" by Senator Mark O. Hatfield. Reprinted by permission of the author.

"Sing a Song of Christmas Carols" by Marjorie Holmes from the anthology *The Meaning of Christmas* compiled by Laura Hobe. Reprinted by permission of Marjorie Holmes.

Library of Congress Cataloging in Publication Data
Main entry under title:

Christmas joys.

"A Doubleday-Galilee original."
1. Christmas. I. Brown, Joan Winmill.
BV45.C575   242′.33
AACR2

ISBN: 0-385-17440-3
Library of Congress Catalog Card Number: 81–43454

CONTENTS

The Joy of Home

The Joy of Children

The Joy of Christmas Fare

The Joy of Giving

The Joy of Music

The Joy of Traditions

INTRODUCTION

Christmas! The very word brings joy to our hearts. No matter how we may dread the rush, the long Christmas lists for gifts and cards to be bought and given—when Christmas Day comes there is still the same warm feeling we had as children, the same warmth that enfolds our hearts and our homes.

All over the world people keep the traditions they learned as children. These links with the past cheer us and bring hope for the years that lie ahead. The unbroken chain that binds us to that first Christmas strengthens our faith.

My search for the best in Christmas literature for this anthology led me to many diverse and interesting sources. The vast and majestic Library of Congress in Washington, D.C., the small friendly local libraries, old bookshops, garage sales, books borrowed from friends, all have kept me finding serendipitous contributions.

As I read over four hundred books, I was led into so many different worlds. From the great halls of England in Henry VIII's time to the present, Christmas surrounded me. Charles Dickens' account of a Victorian Christmas escorted me back through the corridors of the past, so that in my imagination I could experience being a guest at the Cratchits' with

Tiny Tim and share their meager, but nevertheless joyous, Christmas dinner. I was transported to a Christmas of love and selfless giving in New England with Jo and her sisters in Louisa May Alcott's *Little Women*.

Reading about the joy of giving made me reflect on the happiness we receive when we give with a heart of love and reminded me of that great and glorious gift of love that God gave to us that first Christmas. It is in the remembering and the receiving that we are all brought to the deep and lasting reality of God's indescribable gift . . . "a Savior, who is Christ the Lord!" His birthday is a time for us to celebrate this joyous news.

Jesus could have been born in a palace, amid all the finery that befits a king, but He came to us in the lowliness of a stable in Bethlehem, that we might accept Him—whoever we are, in whatever circumstances we find ourselves.

In compiling this book of *Christmas Joys* I have come to appreciate even more this special holiday. Reading so many of the world's finest authors has enriched my life and given me a new awareness of all that Christmas means. We as people may differ outwardly, but inside, each of us longs to be loved and accepted. When we receive God's gift to us, we experience just that.

I would like to express my gratitude to all those who have contributed to *Christmas Joys*. My special thanks to Eve Roshevsky and Peter Schneider whose encouragement and editorial talents have been such a creative part of this book. To my husband Bill, I am deeply grateful for all his patient and loving help.

As you share the joys of the many contributors to this book, may your Christmas be filled with happiness and with the joy of Jesus Christ, and on Christmas morning may the words of Henry Van Dyke enfold you:

The day of joy returns, Father in Heaven,
And crowns another year with peace and goodwill.

JOAN WINMILL BROWN

CHRISTMAS
JOYS

THE JOY
OF
THE SAVIOR

Christmas

FAITH BALDWIN

The snow is full of silver light
Spilled from the heavens' tilted cup
And, on this holy, tranquil night,
The eyes of men are lifted up
To see the promise written fair,
The hope of peace for all on earth,
And hear the singing bells declare
The marvel of the dear Christ's birth.
The way from year to year is long
And though the road be dark so far,
Bright is the manger, sweet the song,
The steeple rises to the Star.

The Prophecy

Isaiah 9:6, 7

For unto us a child is born, unto us a son is given: and the government shall be upon his shoulder: and his name shall be called Wonderful, Counsellor, The mighty God, The everlasting Father, The Prince of Peace. Of the increase of his government and peace there shall be no end, upon the throne of David, and upon his kingdom, to order it, and to establish it with judgment and with justice from henceforth even for ever.

The Purpose of His Coming

WARREN W. WIERSBE

Seven hundred years before Jesus was born, the prophet Isaiah saw Him coming . . . Isaiah saw that this child was unique; He was "born" and He was "given." In other words, this child was both God and man! As God, He was given—the Father's love-gift to a sinful world. This child would be God in human flesh!

What would this child do? He would grow up and one day take the government of mankind upon His shoulder and bring order and peace to a world filled with confusion and war. But before taking the government upon His shoulder, He would first take a cross upon His shoulder, and then die upon that cross, bearing in His body the sins of the world. Before He could wear the diadem of glory as King of Kings, He had to wear a shameful crown of thorns and give His life as a sacrifice for the sins of the world. The kingly Lion of the tribe of Judah first had to come as the lowly Lamb of God, for until sin had been paid for, God's righteous government could not be established.

From *In Memoriam*

ALFRED TENNYSON

The time draws near the birth of Christ:
    The moon is hid; the night is still;
    The Christmas bells from hill to hill
Answer each other in the mist.

Four voices of four hamlets round,
    From far and near, on mead and moor,
    Swell out and fail, as if a door
Were shut between me and the sound:

Each voice four changes on the wind,
    That now dilate, and now decrease,
    Peace and goodwill, goodwill and peace,
Peace and goodwill, to all mankind.

This year I slept and woke with pain,
    I almost wish'd no more to wake,
    And that my hold on life would break
Before I heard those bells again:

But they the troubled spirit rule,
    For they controll'd me when a boy;
    They bring me sorrow touch'd with joy,
The merry, merry bells of Yule.

Christians, Awake

JOHN BYROM

Christians, awake,
Salute the happy morn,
Whereon the Savior of the world was born.

Christmas Peace

CORRIE TEN BOOM

He came, in order that joy would be brought to all the nations, and they would be reconciled with God. He brought peace on earth and wants to bring it also into your soul—that peace which the world cannot give. He is the One who would save His people from their sins.

What Christmas Means to Me

BILLY GRAHAM

The key word of Christmas is Emmanuel—"God with us" (Matthew 1:23). It was as though I, while walking along a road, stepped on an anthill. I might look down and say to the ants, "I am terribly sorry that I've stepped on your anthill. I've disrupted your home. Everything is in confusion. I wish I could tell you that I loved you, that I did not mean to do it, that I would like to help you."

But you say, "That's absurd, that's impossible; ants cannot understand your language!" That's just it! How wonderful it would be if I could only become an ant for a few moments and in their own language tell them of my love for them!

That, in effect, is what Christ did. He came to reveal God to men. He it is who told us that God loves us and is interested in our lives. He it is who told us of the mercy and long-suffering and grace of God. ". . . not that we loved God, but that He loved us, and sent His Son to be the propitiation for our sins" (1 John 4:10). He it is who promised life everlasting.

But more than that, Jesus Christ partook of flesh and blood in order that He might die. He was manifested to take away our sins. Christ came into this world "to give His life a ransom for many." The very purpose of Christ's coming into the world was that He might offer up His life as a sacrifice for the sins of men. He came to die. This is the heart of Christmas.

The Annunciation

Luke 1:26–31, 38

And in the sixth month the angel Gabriel was sent from God unto a city of Galilee, named Nazareth. To a virgin espoused to a man whose name was Joseph, of the house of David; and the virgin's name was Mary. And the angel came in unto her, and said, Hail, thou that art highly favored, the Lord is with thee: blessed art thou among women. And when she saw him, she was troubled at his saying, and cast in her mind what manner of salutation this should be. And the angel said unto her, Fear not, Mary: for thou hast found favor with God. And, behold, thou shalt conceive in thy womb, and bring forth a son, and shalt call his name Jesus . . . And Mary said, Behold the handmaid of the Lord; be it unto me according to thy word. And the angel departed from her.

From *The Apostles' Creed*

I believe . . . in Jesus Christ, His only Son, our Lord; who was conceived by the Holy Ghost, born of the Virgin Mary . . .

7

The Glorious Birth

Luke 2:1–7

And it came to pass in those days, that there went out a decree from Caesar Augustus, that all the world should be taxed. (And this taxing was first made when Cyrenius was governor of Syria.) And all went to be taxed, everyone into his own city. And Joseph also went up from Galilee, out of the city of Nazareth, into Judaea, unto the city of David, which is called Bethlehem; (because he was of the house and lineage of David:) To be taxed with Mary his espoused wife, being great with child. And so it was, that, while they were there, the days were accomplished that she should be delivered. And she brought forth her firstborn son, and wrapped him in swaddling clothes, and laid him in a manger; because there was no room for them in the inn.

Christ and History

CHARLES H. SPURGEON

Christ is the great central fact in the world's history. To Him everything looks forward or backward. All the lines of history converge upon Him. All the great purposes of God culminate in Him. The greatest and most momentous fact which the history of the world records is the fact of His birth.

Christ's Birth: A Necessary Event
on God's Calendar

REV. ERWIN LUTZER

God supervises history! It came about in those days that a decree went out from Caesar Augustus, that a census be taken of the whole inhabited earth. In Roman times, when a decree went out, often it was for one of two reasons: for those available for military service or for the purpose of taxation. Since the Jews were exempt from military service, they felt the reason this decree went out was for the purpose of taxes.

Archaeologists in Egypt and in other places have dug up ancient papyrus manuscripts and on them there are actually copies of decrees that were issued in those days.

In one of the decrees it mentions specifically that everyone should go back to the town of their birth. That's what you have happening here—Joseph had been born in Bethlehem, but because he was a carpenter there was probably a building boom in Nazareth and he had gone there. The decree specified that everyone was to go back to their roots, back to their origins. Thus, the Bible says that Joseph leaves Nazareth and goes to Bethlehem.

Who is it that issued the decree? It was none other than Caesar Augustus, who ruled for about forty-three years. He inherited a vast empire. The Roman Empire was like a huge spider's web, and its roads encompassed the whole earth. Caesar Augustus was the spider and he had everything under his control. This was a very *ordinary* event. He sent out a decree that all the world should be enrolled and the machinery of this great world power was set in motion.

I want you to see something. When God had to get a Virgin from Nazareth to Bethlehem to fulfill prophecy, He used the decree of a pagan king to get her there . . . because *God supervises history!* In that great dramatic moment, when the great mystery of Godliness was going to take place and the Son of God was about to be born, because *God had spoken*—Rome had to cooperate with Bethlehem. Caesar had to be in tune with Jesus; and the purposes of the nations had to be brought in line with God's purpose for Israel.

Why? Because four hundred and fifty years earlier God had spoken, "But thou, Bethlehem Ephratah, though thou be little among the thousands of Judah, yet out of thee shall he come forth unto me that is to be ruler in Israel; whose goings forth have been from of old, from everlasting" (Micah 5:2). And the Virgin had to be in Bethlehem on time . . . God supervises history!

God with Us

Matthew 1:22, 23

Now all this was done, that it might be fulfilled which was spoken of the Lord by the prophet, saying, Behold, a virgin shall be with child, and shall bring forth a son, and they shall call his name Emmanuel, which being interpreted is, God with us.

Bethlehem

Matthew 2:6

Bethlehem in the land of Judah, you are far from least in the eyes of the rulers of Judah; for out of you shall come a leader to be the shepherd of my people Israel.

The Joy of the Savior

ROBERT BROWNING

I never realized God's birth before,
How he grew likest God in being born.
. . . .
Such ever was love's way—to rise, it stoops.

From *The Life of Christ*

FULTON J. SHEEN

Joseph was full of expectancy as he entered the city of his family, and was quite convinced that he would have no difficulty in finding lodgings for Mary, particularly on account of her condition. Joseph went from house to house only to find each one crowded. He searched in vain for a place where He, to Whom heaven and earth belonged, might be born. Could it be that the Creator would not find a home in creation? Up a steep hill Joseph climbed to a faint light which swung on a rope across a doorway. This would be the village inn. There, above all other places, he would surely find shelter. There was room in the inn for the soldiers of Rome who had brutally subjugated the Jewish people; there was room for the daughters of the rich merchants of the East; there was room for those clothed in soft garments, who lived in the houses of the king; in fact, there was room for anyone who had a coin to give the innkeeper; but there was no room for Him Who came to be the Inn of every homeless heart in the world. When finally the scrolls of history are completed down to the last words in time, the saddest line of all will be: "There was no room in the inn."

Out to the hillside to a stable cave, where shepherds sometimes drove their flocks in time of storm, Joseph and Mary went at last for shelter. There, in a place of peace in the lonely abandonment of a cold windswept cave; there, under the floor of the world, He Who is born without a mother in heaven, is born without a father on earth.

Of every other child that is born into the world, friends can say that it resembles his mother. This was the first instance in time that anyone could say that the mother resembled the child. This is the beautiful paradox of the child who made His mother; the mother, too, was only a child. It was also the first time in the history of this world that anyone could ever think of heaven as being anywhere else than "somewhere up there"; when the child was in her arms, Mary now looked down to Heaven.

From *Two from Galilee*

MARJORIE HOLMES

He turned and looked a moment at the manger. "This is our cross, Mary. Yours and mine—for you know how much I love Him too. But this is our cross—to know that our son's hour will come and we can't stop it. To live with that certainty every day of our lives. But this is our blessing," he told her. "To know that in His living and His dying He will be lifting the yoke somewhere for all men. Life with its burdens will be more tolerable. There will be hope. Not only for the freedom of Israel, our own people, but all people who are enslaved.

"And hope for the tormented spirit, Mary. To have some link, some proof that the God we worship really cares about us. Not to have to *fight* God any more, not to be estranged from Him." Joseph's face was working, he was struggling to make it clear. "That too is suffering, perhaps the worst suffering of all. Somehow through this child all this will come about."

The Christmas Symbol

AUTHOR UNKNOWN

Only a manger, cold and bare,
Only a maiden mild,
Only some shepherds kneeling there,
Watching a little Child;
And yet that maiden's arms enfold
The King of heaven above;
And in the Christ-Child we behold
The Lord of Life and Love.

Mary Remembers

JOAN WINMILL BROWN

He was my son.

I loved Him from the moment I saw Him, so small and vulnerable in the manger.

As I looked at His little face, I remembered when the angel came to tell me I would bear a child and that His name would be Jesus, the Son of God. I was only a teenage girl—why had I been selected for this honor? I felt so unworthy.

How kind Joseph was—his faith in me when others doubted helped through the months that lay ahead. His tenderness made the long journey to Bethlehem easier to bear. I shall always remember his expression of concern as he went from place to place looking for lodgings for us and, finding none, had to finally settle for the stable.

It was not easy to bear a child away from my family, without the help of a kindly woman and in such surroundings: but Joseph's love and gentleness and the knowledge that this was God's child helped to erase the pain.

Jesus lay in my arms, warm and sleeping, after we had wrapped Him in swaddling clothes. I looked at this beautiful child not knowing all there would be to face, but thanking God for the gift He had sent.

As we had reached the hill overlooking Bethlehem, I had felt such a feeling of thankfulness that the long journey was over; but the journey through Jesus' life was only just beginning. As He grew He was so different from my other children . . . He always seemed to have a purpose to His life, even when He was very small. His knowledge of the scriptures amazed everyone.

That day as I looked into His face as a baby, I could not have borne the terrible anguish and pain if I had known that one day I would see Him hanging on a cross . . . crucified. I thank God that when that excruciating moment came He gave me the grace to bear it.

How I loved Him, for He was my son. I loved Him as all mothers love their sons, with all the memories of His childhood flooding through my mind.

But most of all I love Him because He was sent from God. In that indisputable fact I have shed my grief, as I look to Him for strength throughout my earthly days and for the promise of eternal life.

One day Jesus will be there to shepherd me across that unknown moment . . . at His appointed time. Not because He was my son, but because He is our Savior!

Love Came Down at Christmas

CHRISTINA G. ROSSETTI

Love came down at Christmas,
Love all lovely, Love Divine;
Love was born at Christmas,
Star and Angels gave the sign.

Worship we the Godhead,
Love Incarnate, Love Divine;
Worship we our Jesus:
But wherewith for sacred sign?

Love shall be our token,
Love be yours and love be mine,
Love to God and all men,
Love for plea and gift and sign.

The Boy and the Crèche

THE REVEREND CLARKE KIMBERLY OLER

There he was again. He was barely six years old and wearing his red knit stocking hat, his face pressed against the iron fence which surrounds the garden of the Church of the Holy Trinity in New York City. It was not usual for a child so young to be out on the streets alone, and I had seen this little boy before. He always wore the same grimy red hat pulled over his ears, the same old sneakers, the same tattered jacket. Several times I had spoken to him, trying to find out who he was, but each time he had just looked at me with large solemn eyes which, together with his small grim mouth, conveyed a smoldering distrust. Without a word he had run off down the street and disappeared.

It was Christmas Eve. The snow had been falling all day and I was looking out the window of the rectory, taking the measure of the snowfall and calculating how much shoveling I would have to do before the people started arriving for the midnight service. The street was deserted; the church garden was dark; a single street lamp poked feeble beams through the foggy night which reflected off the great glistening Gothic gateposts now sporting white tam-o'-shanters of snow.

The only bright spot on the street shone from the huge Nativity scene erected in the church garden. Life-sized figures of the shepherds and kings and barnyard animals attended a lifelike figure of the baby Jesus. The stable, made of folding pieces of plywood, was painted with realistic beams and cobwebs. And on the ground surrounding the manger was a thick covering of real straw. The figure of Mary knelt by the manger, tenderly contemplating the Holy Child.

Then it was that I saw him again—with that unmistakable red hat—his cheeks and nose almost as red as his hat from the cold—peering through the fence at the crèche. As I watched, the small boy ventured timidly through the church gate and across the fresh snow. For a long moment he stood before the crèche. Suddenly he climbed inside . . . and curled up in the straw. Every now and then someone would pass by on the street but no one noticed the little boy curled up under the gentle gaze of the Virgin Mary.

For half an hour I watched, not daring to go outside because I knew that the moment I opened the door he would scamper away. Now and again, when there was no one passing by, I could see a little arm reach up and small fingers would touch the cheek of the Virgin . . . Then something startled him. In a flash he was up, out the gate and down the street. He disappeared into the night.

I felt as though I had been granted a momentary look into a lonely child's heart. I ached for him. I felt utterly helpless. All I could do was breathe a prayer that somehow the Blessed Virgin had managed to comfort him with her unperturbed tenderness and her unchanging expression of love.

Aren't we all like that little boy? Are we not specks on a tiny planet lost in the trackless dark of space? Do we not look up into the empty heavens with brave eyes which conceal anxious hearts? And do we not reach out, in our imaginations, to touch with aching fingers the loving cheek of God? Every Christmas my thoughts return to that boy. I wonder what has become of him. I wonder whether somewhere some loving human hands have reached out to him in place of the crèche figure of the Virgin Mary.

A Christmas Message

CASPER TEN BOOM

If the inhabitants of Bethlehem had known who Joseph and Mary were and who the little child was who would be born of her—how gladly would they have prepared a little place for Him! But as it was then, it often is today. Many leave the Savior, who is knocking, standing at the door of their heart, without paying attention to Him. For they have no place for Jesus. Many are too busy with themselves, and do not believe that He is the Son of the living God . . .

It is told that Victoria, the Queen of England, when staying at her summer residence, Balmoral, likes to take long walks through the woods in simple clothes, and has pleasure in remaining unknown. Some years ago, she was caught in a heavy rainstorm while on one of these trips.

Noticing an old cottage, she ran toward it for refuge. In this cottage lived an old peasant woman alone, who left her house only to take care of her goat and tend her small garden.

The Queen greeted her and kindly asked if she could borrow an umbrella. She added that she would take care to have it returned soon to its owner. The old woman had never seen the Queen, and so she had no idea who she could be.

Therefore she answered in a grudging tone, "Well, I have two umbrellas. One is very good and almost new. I have used it very little. The other one is very worn and has had its time. You may take the old one; the new one I don't lend to anybody—for who knows whether I would ever get it back?" With these words, she gave the Queen the old umbrella, which was torn and battered with spokes sticking out on all sides.

The Queen thought, With this kind of weather, a bad umbrella is better than nothing at all, and accepted it politely. Thanking the woman, she left smiling.

But how great was the horror of the poor old woman when the next morning, a servant in royal livery entered and returned to her the old umbrella in the name of Queen Victoria—with her thanks—and the assurance that Her Majesty had received good service from it! How sorry she was that she had not offered to the Queen the very best she had, and over and over she cried out, "If only I had known! Oh, if only I would have known!"

This will also be the cry of those who will realize too late who *He* is in the day when all eyes will see Him.

Were Earth a Thousand Times as Fair

MARTIN LUTHER

Were earth a thousand times as fair,
Beset with gold and jewels rare,
She yet were far too poor to be
A narrow cradle, Lord, for Thee.

The Messengers of God

Luke 2:8–14

And there were in the same country shepherds abiding in the field, keeping watch over their flock by night. And, lo, the angel of the Lord came upon them, and the glory of the Lord shone round about them: and they were sore afraid. And the angel said unto them, Fear not: for, behold, I bring you good tidings of great joy, which shall be to all people. For unto you is born this day in the city of David a Savior, which is Christ the Lord. And this shall be a sign unto you; Ye shall find the babe wrapped in swaddling clothes, lying in a manger. And suddenly there was with the angel a multitude of the heavenly host praising God, and saying, Glory to God in the highest and on earth peace, goodwill toward men.

The Shepherds Hear

PHILLIP KELLER

The shepherds, on that still night, standing awestruck under the desert skies, knew fully what the angel's message meant. They may have been simple plain men but they were informed men saturated in the teachings of the Scriptures of the Old Testament prophets. And the significance of the events that night was not wasted on them.

Quickly they gathered together, forgetting their flocks for the present, and hurried to the stables in Bethlehem. A quick search soon led them to where the newborn babe lay cradled in a manger. Being good-hearted, generous country folk, they no doubt heaped their hearty congratulations on Joseph and Mary in awe and wonder. They would tell ecstatically but with restrained excitement about the visit and proclamation of the angel and his attendant choir.

In the bighearted, happy way that sheepmen have, they would insist that Mary and Joseph bring their tiny mite of a newborn child into one of their own humble homes. Not for another hour would they think of leaving their newfound friends in the stable with all its stench and filth.

Excitedly the good news swept along the shepherd lines of communication. Each shared with others the happy news of what had happened in and around the tiny town of Bethlehem that night. Visitors came by the score, bearing their simple birthday gifts of white milk, white cheese, white wool, and perhaps even the odd white lamb.

These were but tokens of esteem and gratitude to the Lord God who alone could bestow on them the gift of His own Lamb.

The Manger's Message

B. CLAYTON BELL

Let's hear some of the things that the manger says to us at this Christmas time.

The first thing the manger says to us is something about the love of God. The manger tells us again that the kind of place for which God is looking is not necessarily beautiful and appealing. Rather, God is looking for a place that will receive Him. He does not look for the beauty of sainthood. What He is looking for is needy sinners. He can do nothing for the person who is intent on being self-righteous. Jesus said as much later on, "I am not come to call the righteous, but sinners to repentance." He said, "I have come to seek and to save the lost." If nothing else, the manger ought to remind us that what God is looking for is not perfection. God is not looking for a place to stay that is neatly scrubbed and clean and perfect.

The second thing that I think we can hear the manger saying to us is this: availability is nine tenths of usefulness. It was there and so God used it. With all of the rush of Christmas and with all of the activity of our modern world, it is so easy to push God out of the picture. But God simply is looking for availability. And we *can* be available, if we will be. There is room in your inn. You just simply have to find it and make it available.

The innkeeper had crowded out the birth of the Christ child, but a lowly manger was available and God took that opportunity.

What room do you have for Him? It doesn't have to be neatly scrubbed, cleaned and antiseptic. It simply needs an open door through which He can walk.

19

From *My Favorite Christmas Story*

ROY ROGERS

After Mary and Joseph, the animals in the stable were the first to see Him, in His swaddling clothes. Maybe there was a young calf there, and maybe that reminded the Jews in the inn that His people had once worshiped a golden calf. Or an ox: there were some people who worshiped oxen. Or a sheep, marked for sacrifice that week in the Temple at Jerusalem. But now that the Baby had come the sacrifice of animals was on the way out; men would not worship or sacrifice beasts any more; they would worship the Christ who lay in the straw. The breath and the warm bodies of the animals warmed Him, in the little room. If they could have talked, what would they have said to Him? What would the lambs have said to the Lamb of God who would be sacrificed on a cross?

The animals—then the shepherds from the hills. The shepherds were the first men to come. The people in the courtyard may have looked in at Him, and smiled, and gone away never knowing what they had seen, but the shepherds *came,* and they came because they knew, and they came to worship. Out on their hillsides, watching their sheep, they had heard a great strange music. If *you* will go out this Christmas Eve and stand still and just look up at the stars, and listen, you can hear it, too—the music that comes from behind the stars, from another world. You can hear it, if you'll listen.

The shepherds heard the angels sing: "Glory to God in the highest, and on earth peace, goodwill . . ." Peace? For the shepherds, who got kicked around by everybody? Goodwill? Who had anything good to say about a shepherd? You were really out of luck, if you had to watch sheep for a living; that was about as far down as you could go. But my Bible says the shepherds heard it first, and that they came first to worship the little King who would make them the equals of anyone in the world. They had waited a long, long time for this night—ever since Abraham was a shepherd in Ur, ever since David was a shepherd in Bethlehem, they had waited. Now they came running into Bethlehem, *believing what the angels had told them.* They came first because they were the first to understand that this was the Good Shepherd . . .

They were poor, so they couldn't have brought any Christmas presents —oh, maybe a little milk, or wool, or a baby lamb. But their gifts weren't important. *They brought themselves.* It was all the Baby would have wanted from them. Did you ever stop to think, at Christmas, that the only gift He wants from you is you?

Christmas is giving time—time for giving ourselves.

We don't think enough about those shepherds. We talk about how they came to Bethlehem; how about looking at how they *left* Bethlehem? They left it "glorifying and praising God"—and man, that's important. I'll bet they sang all the way home. Anyone who meets Jesus Christ goes away singing. It's a little like going to church; you can't go there without feeling better.

Something happened to the shepherds. They didn't go home and sit around the rest of their lives dreaming about what happened that night. They told everybody about it, and "all they who heard it wondered." It figures. They had to tell everybody. I never knew a happy man who was a quiet man, who could keep his mouth shut about whatever it is that is making him happy.

Christmas is telling time—wondering time. Wonder enough about it, and you'll know, and you'll tell about it . . .

The Story of the Wise Men

Matthew 2:1, 2, 7–11

Now when Jesus was born in Bethlehem of Judaea in the days of Herod the king, behold, there came wise men from the east to Jerusalem, Saying, Where is he that is born King of the Jews? for we have seen his star in the east, and are come to worship him . . . Then Herod, when he had privily called the wise men, inquired of them diligently what time the star appeared. And he sent them to Bethlehem and said, Go and search diligently for the young child; and when ye have found him, bring me word again, that I may come and worship him also. When they had heard the king, they departed; and lo, the star, which they saw in the east, went before them, till it came and stood over where the young child was. When they saw the star, they rejoiced with exceeding great joy. And when they were come into the house, they saw the young child with Mary his mother, and fell down, and worshiped him: and when they had opened their treasures, they presented unto him gifts; gold, and frankincense, and myrrh.

The Nativity

C. S. LEWIS

Among the oxen (like an ox I'm slow)
I see a glory in the stable grow
Which, with the ox's dullness might at length
    Give me an ox's strength.

Among the asses (stubborn I as they)
I see my Savior where I looked for hay;
So may my beastlike folly learn at least
    The patience of a beast.

Among the sheep (I like a sheep have strayed)
I watch the manger where my Lord is laid;
Oh that my baa-ing nature would win thence
    Some woolly innocence!

The Three Kings

HENRY WADSWORTH LONGFELLOW

Three Kings came riding from far away,
    Melchior and Gaspar and Baltasar;
Three Wise Men out of the East were they,
And they traveled by night and they slept by day,
    For their guide was a beautiful, wonderful star.

The star was so beautiful, large and clear,
    That all the other stars of the sky
Became a white mist in the atmosphere;
And by this they knew that the coming was near
    Of the Prince foretold in the prophecy.

The Gift of Love

John 1:1–5, 11–14

In the beginning was the Word, and the Word was with God, and the Word was God. The same was in the beginning with God. All things were made by him; and without him was not any thing made that was made. In him was life; and the life was the light of men. And the light shineth in darkness; and the darkness comprehended it not . . . He came unto his own, and his own received him not. But as many as received him, to them gave he power to become the sons of God, even to them that believe on his name: Which were born, not of blood, nor of the will of the flesh, nor of the will of man, but of God. And the Word was made flesh, and dwelt among us, (and we beheld his glory, the glory as of the only begotten of the Father,) full of grace and truth.

The Living Word

MARK O. HATFIELD, UNITED STATES SENATOR

The word was made flesh. Christ came to a real world of political upheaval, social turmoil, human suffering and spiritual blindness. His life and His ministry were relevant to all those situations. And therefore, the sharing of His life must be related to all these conditions as they are in our society today. We must see what we are to be saved *from* and what we are redeemed and liberated by Christ *for*. The false dichotomy between the personal and the social must be destroyed. The notion that being evangelical means that one does not have to concern himself with social problems, or that ministering to social ills is different from an evangelical concern is simply heretical, whichever way you look at it. I believe our task is to restore the whole Gospel. Sin is both corporate and personal, and usually both at the same time. The coming of Christ speaks both to our personal lives and to our corporate structures, just as it did in Palestine two thousand years ago.

Don't Miss the Joy!

LLOYD JOHN OGILVIE

Joy is the outer expression of the inner experience of being loved. Robert Louis Stevenson was right. "To miss the joy is to miss all." I have a friend who has a favorite saying each time he closes a conversation and says good-bye. He takes ahold of a person's hand and says, "Don't miss the joy!" Not a bad Christmas Day greeting for friends and loved ones. A sure sign that we have allowed Christmas to happen to us is an artesian joy which lasts all through the year.

Joy is not gush or ho-ho jolliness. Joy grows in the assurance that God will use everything that happens to or around us for our ultimate good and for His glory. True joy is what Paul calls a fruit of the Spirit; a result of the Lord living in us. We sing the familiar carol's words: "O come to us, be born in us, O Christ Immanuel." The experience which changes everything is not only accepting the love of Christ's birth in Bethlehem, but opening our hearts for Him to be born in us today. It's one thing to believe in Christ, quite another to receive His indwelling presence. The Lord himself made the promise, "I will make my home in you." "Abide in me and I in you." Life in Christ is claiming Him as Lord and Savior; life with Christ in us is the source of joy! Jesus said, "I came that you may have life and have it more abundantly." The abundant life is life with Christ abiding in us. The Lord's own word is, "These things have I spoken to you that my joy may remain in you, and that your joy may be full" (John 15:11).

The authentic mark of a Christian is joy. More than circumstantial or dependent on people's attitude or words, joy is constant and consistent in life's changing problems. It is unassailable and vibrant. "Joy to the world! the Lord is come." And comes to each of us. And for those who will receive Him, joyous resilience in spite of everything! Don't miss this joy!

A Christmas Prayer

ROBERT LOUIS STEVENSON

Loving Father, help us remember the birth of Jesus, that we may share in the song of the angels, the gladness of the shepherds, and the worship of the wise men.

Close the door of hate and open the door of love all over the world.

Let kindness come with every gift and good desires with every greeting.

Deliver us from evil by the blessing which Christ brings, and teach us to be merry with clear hearts.

May the Christmas morning make us happy to be Thy children, and the Christmas evening bring us to our beds with grateful thoughts, forgiving and forgiven, for Jesus' sake. Amen!

Joy to the World!

ISAAC WATTS

Joy to the world! the Lord is come:
Let earth receive her King;
Let ev'ry heart prepare Him room,
And Heav'n and nature sing.

He rules the world with truth and grace,
And makes the nations prove
The glories of His righteousness,
And wonders of His love.

Christmas Everywhere

PHILLIPS BROOKS

Everywhere, everywhere, Christmas tonight!
Christmas in lands of the fir-tree and pine,
Christmas in lands of the palm-tree and vine,
Christmas where snow-peaks stand solemn and white,
Christmas where cornfields stand sunny and bright,
  Everywhere, everywhere, Christmas tonight!

Christmas where children are hopeful and gay,
Christmas where old men are patient and gray,
Christmas where peace like a dove in his flight,
Broods o'er brave men in the thick of the fight;
  Everywhere, everywhere, Christmas tonight!

For the Christ-child who comes is the Master of all;
No palace too great, no cottage too small . . .

Wonderful

FRANCES RIDLEY HAVERGAL

His name shall be called Wonderful
Isaiah 9:6

All the other names of Jesus are nouns. But here is a name that is an adjective; so we may use it not only as a name by itself, but as an adjective to all His other names; and the more we know Him and love Him the more we shall delight in this.

If we know Jesus as our Savior at all, we shall be quite sure that He is a Wonderful Savior. And if we grow in grace and in the knowledge of our Lord and Savior Jesus Christ, we shall find more and more, year by year, and even day by day, what a Wonderful Friend, and Wonderful Gift, and Wonderful High Priest, and Wonderful everything else He is. . . .

On the Morning of Christ's Nativity

JOHN MILTON

This is the month, and this the happy morn,
Wherein the Son of Heaven's eternal King,
Of wedded maid and virgin mother born,
Our great redemption from above did bring;
For so the holy sages once did sing,
*   That He our deadly forfeit should release;*
And with His father work us a perpetual peace . . .

THE JOY
OF
HOME

At Christmas the Heart Goes Home

MARJORIE HOLMES

At Christmas all roads lead home.

The filled planes, packed trains, overflowing buses, all speak elo-quently of a single destination: home. Despite the crowding and the crushing, the delays, the confusion, we clutch our bright packages and beam our anticipation. We are like birds driven by an instinct we only faintly understand—the hunger to be with our own people.

If we are already snug by our own fireside surrounded by growing children, or awaiting the return of older ones who are away, then the heart takes a side trip. In memory we journey back to the Christmases of long ago. Once again we are curled into quivering balls of excitement listening to the mysterious rustle of tissue paper and the tinkle of untold treasures as parents perform their magic on Christmas Eve. Or we recall the special Christmases that are like little landmarks in the life of a fam-ily.

One memory is particularly dear to me—a Christmas during the Great Depression when Dad was out of work and the rest of us were scattered, struggling to get through school or simply to survive. My sister Gwen and her schoolteacher husband, on his first job in another state, were ex-pecting their first baby. My brother Harold, an aspiring actor, was trav-eling with a road show. I was a senior working my way through a small college five hundred miles away. My boss had offered me fifty dollars—a fortune!—just to keep the office open the two weeks he and his wife would be gone.

"And boy, do I need the money! Mom, I know you'll understand," I wrote.

I wasn't prepared for her brave if wistful reply. The other kids couldn't make it either! Except for my kid brother Barney, she and Dad would be alone. "This house is going to seem empty, but don't worry—we'll be okay."

I did worry, though. Our first Christmas apart! And as the carols drifted up the stairs, as the corridors rang with the laughter and chatter of other girls packing up to leave, my misery deepened.

Then one night when the dorm was almost empty I had a long-distance call. "Gwen!" I gasped. "What's wrong?" (Long-distance usually meant an emergency back in those days.)

"Listen, Leon's got a new generator and we think the old jalopy can make it home. I've wired Harold—if he can meet us halfway, he can ride with us. But don't tell the folks; we want to surprise them. Marj, you've just got to come, too."

"But I haven't got a dime for presents!"

"Neither have we. Cut up a catalog and bring pictures of all the goodies you'd buy if you could—and will someday!"

"I could do that, Gwen. But I just can't leave here now."

When we hung up I reached for the scissor. Furs and perfume. Wristwatches, clothes, cars—how all of us longed to lavish beautiful things on those we loved. Well, at least I could mail mine home—with IOUs.

I was still dreaming over this "wish list" when I was called to the phone again. It was my boss, saying he'd decided to close the office after all. My heart leaped up, for if it wasn't too late to catch a ride as far as Fort Dodge with the girl down the hall . . . ! I ran to pound on her door.

They already had a load, she said—but if I was willing to sit on somebody's lap . . . Her dad was downstairs waiting. I threw things into a suitcase, then rammed a hand down the torn lining of my coat sleeve so fast it emerged mittened and I had to start over.

It was snowing as we piled into that heater-less car. We drove all night with the side curtains flapping, singing and hugging each other to keep warm. Not minding—how could we? We were going home!

"Marj!" Mother stood at the door clutching her robe about her, silver-black hair spilling down her back, eyes large with alarm, then incredulous joy. "Oh . . . Marj."

I'll never forget those eyes or the feel of her arms around me, so soft and warm after the bitter cold. My feet felt frozen after that all-night drive, but they warmed up as my parents fed me and put me to bed. And when I woke up hours later it was to the jangle of sleigh bells Dad hung on the door each year. And voices. My kid brother shouting, "Harold! Gwen!" The clamor of astonished greetings, the laughter, the kissing, the questions. And we all gathered around the kitchen table the way we used to, recounting our adventures.

"I had to hitchhike clear to Peoria," my older brother scolded merrily. "Me, the leading man . . ." He lifted an elegant two-toned shoe—with a flapping sole. "In these!"

"But by golly, you got here." Dad's chubby face was beaming. Then suddenly he broke down—Dad, who never cried. "We're together!"

Together. The best present we could give one another, we realized. All of us, just being here in the old house where we'd shared so many Christmases. No gift on our lavish lists, if they could materialize, could equal that.

In most Christmases since that memorable one we've been lucky. During the years our children were growing up there were no separations. Then one year, appallingly, history repeated itself. For valid reasons, not a single faraway child could get home. Worse, my husband had flown to Florida for some vital surgery. A proud, brave man—he was adamant about our not coming with him "just because it's Christmas," when he'd be back in another week.

Like my mother before me, I still had one lone chick left—Melanie, fourteen. "We'll get along fine," she said, trying to cheer me.

We built a big fire every evening, went to church, wrapped presents, pretended. But the ache in our hearts kept swelling. And, the day before Christmas, we burst into mutual tears. "Mommy, it's just not right for Daddy to be down there alone!"

"I know it." Praying for a miracle, I ran to the telephone. The airlines were hopeless, but there was one roomette available on the last train to Miami. Almost hysterical with relief, we threw things into bags.

And what a Christmas Eve! Excited as conspirators, we cuddled together in that cozy space. Melanie hung a tiny wreath in the window and we settled down to watch the endless pageantry flashing by to the rhythmic clicking song of the rails.

. . . Little villages and city streets—all dancing with lights and decorations and sparkling Christmas trees . . . And cars and snowy countrysides and people—all the people. Each one on his or her special pilgrimage of love and celebration this precious night.

At last we drifted off to sleep. But hours later I awoke to a strange stillness. The train had stopped. And, raising the shade, I peered out on a very small town. Silent, deserted, with only a few lights still burning. And under the bare branches, along a lonely street, a figure was walking. A young man in sailor blues, head bent, hunched under the weight of the seabag on his shoulders. And I thought—home! Poor kid, he's almost home. And I wondered if there was someone still up waiting for him; or

33

if anyone knew he was coming at all. And my heart cried out to him, for he was suddenly my own son—and my own ghost, and the soul of us all —driven, so immutably driven by this annual call, "Come home!"

Home for Christmas. There must be some deep psychological reason why we turn so instinctively toward home at this special time. Perhaps we are acting out the ancient story of a man and a woman and a coming child, plodding along with their donkey toward their destination. It was necessary for Joseph, the earthly father, to go home to be taxed. Each male had to return to the city of his birth.

Birth. The tremendous miracle of birth shines through every step and syllable of the Bible story. The long, arduous trip across the mountains of Galilee and Judaea was also the journey of a life toward birth. Mary was already in labor when they arrived in Bethlehem, so near the time of her delivery that in desperation, since the inn was full, her husband settled for a humble stable.

The Child Who was born on that first Christmas grew up to be a man. Jesus. He healed many people, taught us many important things. But the message that has left the most lasting impression and given the most hope and comfort is this: that we do have a home to go to, and there will be an ultimate homecoming. A place where we will indeed be reunited with those we love.

Anyway, that's my idea of heaven. A place where Mother is standing in the door, probably bossing Dad the way she used to about the turkey or the tree, and he's enjoying every minute of it. And old friends and neighbors are streaming in and out and the sense of love and joy and celebration will go on forever.

A place where every day will be Christmas, with everybody there together. At home.

Room at the Inn

LAUREL LEE

It began to look as if we wouldn't have Christmas anywhere but in our little stable. Last year I had been full term into my pregnancy with Mary Elisabeth. The line I held close from the Christmas story had been "She was great with child." I had identified with Mary because she was fat, and so was I. This year I could only think of her accommodations.

I was living with my three children, alone, in the upstairs apartment of an old house. I moved in after a year of having everything I knew subtracted from me. A routine prenatal checkup revealed Hodgkin's disease, which led to a series of hospitalizations and radiation treatments.

I had to work on my attitude because in the attitude is the battle, not in the circumstance itself. Self-pity could come and whisper "follow me," but I girded my mind and refused to make a Kleenex box my centerpiece.

The small apartment where we lived called for an exercise in the new math—how to divide the four of us into one bedroom. I collapsed the Port-A-Crib through the doorway of the living room closet for eleven-month-old Mary Elisabeth. I explained to Matthew, who was six, that his bedroom was going to be like a train berth six feet above my own bed. I folded a sleeping bag to equal the two-board width of the closet shelf and covered this makeshift mattress with a sheet. Once I mounted a paper locomotive on the inside of his door, Matthew climbed up into his "berth" with a flashlight and was home. As for five-year-old Anna, she and her extended family of stuffed bears slept with me.

Then in late autumn a "for sale" sign, built like a bell, was planted near the porch of a house across the street. The residing family had lived there for twenty years, and the real estate agent explained to me that their move was contingent on the house they were purchasing.

When I asked what the price was, I was delighted to hear a figure that was possible. I followed through with all the business of a buyer and even led the children in a victory parade through the new backyard, around the apple trees. Mary Elisabeth was our one float in her portable stroller.

I was so anxious to move that every time I opened a closet I imagined I was shaking hands with the doorknob to say "good-bye." Our new home would have bedrooms for all of us!

But with the advent of winter, my neighbors still hadn't moved. I watched the house with the intensity of a bird watcher. I wanted to see a nest of cardboard boxes. But there was never any activity.

I went to the doctor for my winter checkup. A radiation waiting room can have the same quality of silence as an elevator full of people who won't talk to each other. Some clinician had covered three cardboard circles with cotton swabs and joined them together into the snowman pattern.

The fact that I felt fine is not the whole evidence in the cancer department. I complied with the chest X ray, the blood work and the examination. The laboratory reports were available that afternoon.

"Everything is normal and healthy," said the doctor. He went on to quote Benjamin Franklin: "God does the healing, and the doctor collects the fee." I felt like rushing out into the street and shaking hands with everyone.

There is a time line to Christmas. My first deadline was Christmas cards. The exchange of them was my special winter garden. They were cast out like seeds in white envelopes, and I harvested their return in my mailbox. Bringing in the Christmas tree was our centerfold in preparing for Christmas. With it came the box from the storage bins to deck the halls. I liked to wrap my ornaments in the grocery ads to see how much prices had risen over the year.

Decorating the tree is a matter of perception. Matthew and Anna exclusively garnished the branches that were level with their necks. I tried to encourage them to be aware of the tree as a whole. But their frond received thorough and complete attention. Anna rolled tissues and connected them to the tree by forcing the needles through a strategically bit hole. The branch looked as if it was suffering from a very bad cold. Matthew had a number of pictures from school. He decided to mount them on the tree at the three-foot line. Mary Elisabeth could crawl and reach, so the very bottom rim was left absolutely bare. She was delighted all season long with the water in the red metal tree stand.

I popped popcorn and gave Matthew and Anna a thread and needles. They added their four-inch popcorn strings. Our last touch was tinsel.

"It's supposed to look like ice drips," I explained. So, making the sound of a great howling wind, Matthew threw the tinsel because he knew that such ice formations would only come in a storm. Anna joined him like a blue norther, and we were done.

I store presents. Like a squirrel with a good nut, I bury them under my bed. There are occasions all year for giving. Garage sales are my floating bazaar. Little children don't care if a toy is secondhand.

My parents were coming for Christmas. They are the wonderful grandmother and grandfather who arrive in a sleigh of a station wagon.

I have always yearned to find the perfect bumper sticker for them. It would say, "Have you asked us about our grandchildren?" But before they came I had things to do. Housecleaning is done in levels. There is one kind of preparation for a friend and another kind for a mother. One day, while I embroidered a blouse for a gift, the telephone rang with the news that the Wilsons were finally moving. They would vacate the house on December 18. "There's room at the inn," I shouted.

It was a cold Saturday morning as the Wilsons and their friends carried their belongings out the back door. From then on, we never crossed the street with our hands empty. We went to get cartons from the grocery store. Once they were stacked, I balanced them on the stroller handle. Matthew carried his, Anna carried hers, and we looked like three box turtles coming home. We would move by Christmas and give my folks the upstairs apartment.

On Christmas Eve morning I took the ornaments and lights off the tree in order to carry it across the street. It was small but awkward. To any eye other than my children's, it would be an ugly duckling among the Douglas fir swans. It looked so absolutely pathetic that I said, "Tree, you know you smell good."

After the children collapsed into sleep on Christmas Eve night I walked through the whole world of my new home. I was full of the plans that are made in a moment but take months to accomplish. The living room was my only civilized country. I went down into the basement, and under the stairs was a wooden box with rope handles. I loosened it and opened the lid, exposing a layer of Christmas cards on top of old books. There were pages of sheet music. One folder had a lady with a big corsage pinned at her waist, singing, "Joy to the world! The Lord is come." I picked up one small book, attracted by the leather cover embossed with oak leaves and acorns. In a wreath was the title, *Friendship and Character,* by Emerson. On the flyleaf, a man named Teddy had written: "Have a Merry Christmas—December 24, 1914."

The Noel messages seemed to be addressed to me. I know there is an order beyond coincidence. I thought for a moment about the future, and I told myself firmly, I will seize and hold that little phrase, "Happy New Year." I will fold it into my breast pocket, insert it into my right mitten, tuck it under my wool cap.

For a long time I sat on the steps, musing. I thought of long-gone holidays. I stretched back into the wonderland mist. I once got a doll named Mary with a pink and black taffeta bib. I remembered the first bicycle with tires as wide as a man's foot.

I turned upstairs. Tomorrow the floor will disintegrate into a red sea of paper scraps. My father will shoot a whole roll of film, and once developed, some will go to his office, some to my mother's wallet, and one, enlarged, will be sent back to me.

Mother will bake a ruby cake, and I'll insist we handle the whole matter as a birthday party.

Before I went to bed I said a little prayer: This year we have some superior accommodations for you, Lord Jesus. And our hearts have made themselves ready for your day.

Christmas Speech, 1941

WINSTON CHURCHILL

While Winston Churchill was staying at the White House, Christmas 1941—during World War II—he delivered this speech to the American people:

I spend this anniversary and festival far from my country, far from my family, and yet I cannot truthfully say that I feel far from home. Whether it be the ties of blood on my mother's side, or the friendships I have developed here over many years of active life, or the commanding sentiment of comradeship in the common cause of great peoples who speak the same language, who kneel at the same altars and, to a very large extent, pursue the same ideals; I cannot feel myself a stranger here in the center and at the summit of the United States. I feel a sense of unity and fraternal association which, added to the kindliness of your welcome, convinces me that I have a right to sit at your fireside and share your Christmas joys.

Fellow workers, fellow soldiers in the cause, this is a strange Christmas Eve. Almost the whole world is locked in deadly struggle. Armed with the most terrible weapons which science can devise, the nations advance upon each other. Ill would it be for us this Christmastide if we were not sure that no greed for the lands or wealth of any other people, no vulgar ambitions, no morbid lust for material gain at the expense of others had led us to the field. Ill would it be for us if that were so. Here, in the midst of war, raging and roaring over all the lands and seas, sweeping nearer to our hearths and homes; here, amid all these tumults, we have tonight the peace of the spirit in each cottage home and in every generous heart. Therefore we may cast aside, for this night at least, the cares and dangers which beset us and make for the children an evening of happiness in a world of storm. Here then, for one night only, each home throughout the English-speaking world should be a brightly lighted island of happiness and peace.

Let the children have their night of fun and laughter, let the gifts of Father Christmas delight their play. Let us grown-ups share to the full in their unstinted pleasures before we turn again to the stern tasks and the formidable years that lie before us, resolved that by our sacrifice and daring these same children shall not be robbed of their inheritance or denied their right to live in a free and decent world.

And so, in God's mercy, a happy Christmas to you all.

God Bless the Master of This House

Author unknown

God bless the master of this house,
The mistress also,
And all the little children
That round the table go:

And all your kin and kinsfolk
That dwell both far and near;
We wish you a merry Christmas,
And a happy New Year.

From *a letter written by General Robert E. Lee to his wife December 25, 1861*

I cannot let this day of grateful rejoicing pass without some communion with you. I am thankful for the many among the past that I have passed with you, and the remembrance of them fills me with pleasure. As to our old home, if not destroyed it will be difficult ever to be recognized.

. . . It is better to make up our minds to a general loss. They cannot take away the remembrances of the spot, and the memories of those that to us rendered it sacred. That will remain to us as long as life will last and that we can preserve . . .

Christmas in the Heart

Author unknown

It is Christmas in the mansion,
    Yule-log fires and silken frocks:
It is Christmas in the cottage,
    Mother's filling little socks.

It is Christmas on the highway,
    In the thronging, busy mart;
But the dearest, truest Christmas
    Is the Christmas in the heart.

How Far to Bethlehem?

SYLVIA DOOLING

"How far to Bethlehem?" the minister asked,
"Very far," I answered, as my mind seemed so full—
Gifts to buy, costs to consider,
How very far Bethlehem seemed.

"How far to Bethlehem?" ran round in my head.
"Very far," I answered, as I made my way home,
Lunches to make, newspaper to ponder,
How very far Bethlehem seemed.

A friend came to call who needed my time,
Sorrow had entered two lives,
A chill touched the room as we shared a fresh loss,
How very far Bethlehem seemed.

Loss of home? Loss of love?
Loss of all that is warm and safe—
How far to Bethlehem? Oh God, too far,
On this lonely and sad afternoon.

Then suddenly after tragedy was shared
God's name seemed to vanish the gloom,
As Christ's words of hope were briefly discussed
A small light shone through the room.

And this morning, praise God!
A new day began, and a new birth rang out through the skies,
"How far to Bethlehem?" Oh God, not far—
Just a few short blocks across town.

God's Son once again was born in a life
Not heralded by angels, just a small voice,
Crying out for new hope, new life, a new chance.
And Bethlehem came close once again.

What Shall We Do This Christmas?

COLLEEN TOWNSEND EVANS

A few years ago my husband received a call to the National Presbyterian Church in Washington, D.C., and we knew that that year would be our last in La Jolla. Our family gathering would be especially dear to us, for we would carry its memories for a long, long time.

And then we learned that my parents—Grandma and Grandpa Wilhelm—would not be with us. Grandpa had to undergo surgery and would have to spend Christmas Day in a hospital north of Los Angeles. So we mailed our gifts to each other and bit our lips a little in our disappointment.

If it had been just Louis and I at Christmas I would have suggested driving up to Los Angeles and spending the day with Grandpa, but I just couldn't ask our children to do that. The trip took three and a half hours each way, which meant that we would have to be away from home all day, and our sons and daughter so enjoyed being home at Christmas. I knew their friends would be dropping in all day—and that soon our children would be saying good-bye to these friends for at least a long time. So I put the idea out of my mind.

On Christmas morning we did what we always did as a family. We got up very early, had a light breakfast and then we sat around the tree while one of us read the Christmas story from the gospels. Then we opened our presents, hugging and kissing each other for the thoughtfulness and remembered wishes we found wrapped up in the packages. But it wasn't the same without Grandma and Grandpa. We missed them very much. Our tall, long-haired boys were touchingly open about their feelings. "I sure miss Grandpa . . ." "He's so much fun! . . ." "Yeah—he's a real cruiser! . . ." and Andie's sensitive face and the sadness in her large compassionate eyes said more than words.

It was time for me to take the turkey out of the refrigerator and put it in the oven, and I was glad to have an excuse to go into the kitchen because I thought I was going to cry a little. And I honestly don't know which one of our children said it first, but somebody said, "Hey, how would the rest of you feel about driving up to Los Angeles and seeing Grandma and Grandpa?"

Before I reached the kitchen the others agreed.

"Yeah, that's what I'd like to do!"

"Let's drive up and see them."

"It's not the same without them."

The turkey never got out of the refrigerator that Christmas Day. We left it, stuffed, and ready, for another time. We piled into the car. We took along our projector and a few slides from our summer backpacking trip so that we could show them to my parents.

It was a long drive to the hospital and when we got there the corridors were almost empty. Doctors had sent home as many patients as they could, because everyone knows that a hospital is no place to spend the holidays. We found Grandpa's room and looked in. There he was, sitting up in bed, with Grandma in a straight-backed chair by his bedside. When Grandpa saw us, the tears began to roll down his cheeks and he cried like a little boy overwhelmed with a joy that was just too big for him to hold inside himself. He couldn't get over the fact that we—and especially the children—would choose to drive so far to be with him on this day, this year.

We had a wonderful visit and Grandpa kept saying, "This is the best Christmas I've ever had." We talked and laughed and showed our slides on the white hospital walls and reminisced about our summer vacation in the Sierras. We stayed for several hours, and before we left we all joined hands around Grandpa's bed and thanked God for this day when we were able to be together with our loved ones.

When we left Grandpa's room we were hungry so we went downstairs to the hospital cafeteria which was about to close. There was very little food left—some cole slaw, some dishes of gelatin with whipped cream, and a few cartons of milk—and that was our Christmas dinner. I'm sure that everyone felt as I did . . . that it was one of the richest Christmases we'd ever had.

Let Us Keep Christmas

GRACE NOLL CROWELL

Whatever else be lost among the years,
Let us keep Christmas still a shining thing:
Whatever doubts assail us, or what fears,
Let us hold close one day, remembering
Its poignant meaning for the hearts of men.
Let us get back our childlike faith again.

Christmas Eve

KATE DOUGLAS WIGGIN

The door is on the latch tonight,
The hearth-fire is aglow,
I seem to hear soft passing feet—
The Christ child in the snow.

My heart is open wide tonight
For stranger, kith or kin.
I would not bar a single door
Where Love might enter in.

Christ, Immanuel

LLOYD JOHN OGILVIE

Jesus came to save His people from sin. That's the meaning of the name He was given. "You shall call his name Jesus, for he will save his people from their sins." He was Immanuel, God with us. He came not to establish the traditions of a new religion but to get to the inner heart of people's need. His life, message, death and resurrection were to reconcile us with God eternally. And that wondrous process for each of us begins in the healing of our inner selves. Our memories are liberated with forgiveness, our personalities are reformed around the person of Christ Himself, our turbulent drives and needs are satisfied and reordered around His guidance and direction. The heart becomes His home. "The Father and I will make our home in you." The Christmas carol suddenly has meaning, "Where meek souls will receive Him still, the dear Christ enters in." Then we can sing, "O come to us, abide with us, O Christ, Immanuel."

I Know—I've Been Here

LOUIS H. EVANS, JR.

A few weeks ago, at the beginning of the Christmas season, I visited Pittsburgh, Pennsylvania. My family used to live there when I was a boy, but I hadn't been back in many years. I had a wonderful time walking around in some of their famous old department stores—Gimbels, Joseph Horne, Kaufmann's—remembering how I stood on those same street corners as a boy and looked into the brightly decorated windows just abounding with toys and animated figures. How my eyes would widen! And then my parents would take me upstairs to the toy department where I would look at everything. I was especially wild about electric trains! By the time I had walked around for several hours—and I'm amazed at my folks' patience—thinking about the things I would have liked to have had, I was so high on anticipation I could have flown home with very little effort.

And I can still remember the smell of the Christmas tree that was delivered to our house from McCann's food store, and the snow that usually covered the ground, and the big fireplace, and the excitement of opening presents. It was almost more than I could bear!

Now again, at this time of the year, the traffic is heavy—perhaps not so heavy as in some of the other years—but the shopping has started, the invitations to the many parties are fluttering in, there are the long lines for stamps for Christmas cards, the letters to friends, the people who say, "Hey, come over for a bit of Christmas cheer!"—which usually means the kind of "cheer" poured from a bottle, as though other kinds of cheer were in short supply.

I always feel a little sad when I hear the song that used to be sung:

> *Good Christian men, rejoice,*
> *With heart, and soul, and voice;*
> *Give ye heed to what we say,*
> *Jesus Christ was born to save.*
> *He has ope'd the heavenly door,*
> *Now ye need not fear the grave.*
> *Christ was born to save!*
> *Christ was born to save!*

How out of tune this song seems with so much of the "cheer" that we see during Christmastime . . . the mercantilism, the drinking, the party-

45

ing. And I wonder if we ought to stop the merry-go-round long enough to ask the question, "Well, what is Christmas all about?"

Why did Jesus really come?

We can find one of the reasons in a beautiful passage from the Letter to the Hebrews: "Since therefore the children share in flesh and blood, he himself likewise partook of the same nature . . . he had to be made like his brethren in every respect, so that he might become a merciful and faithful high priest in the service of God" (2:14, 17).

A little further on the writer continues the theme: "For we have not an high priest which cannot be touched with the feelings of our infirmities; but was in all points tempted like as we are, yet without sin. Let us therefore come boldly unto the throne of grace, that we may obtain mercy, and find grace to help in time of need" (Hebrews 4:15, 16).

Why did Christ come? God came to be with us. He came to share this experience of human living in Jesus Christ!

How often, in the midst of pain, struggle, or sorrow, do we feel abject loneliness, the loneliness of being unique. "I'm the only one who's ever gone through this. Nobody could really understand what I'm going through." And in our loneliness we wallow in despair, convinced that no one really understands.

And quite often there's some data to support that conviction. We put up our flag of distress as a friend walks by—but instead of asking us what's wrong, or why we hurt, he says, "Hi, sport, how're you doin'?"— not seriously asking the question. If he had, he would have seen the pain on our face and stopped. But he walks by, his clicking brogue heels hitting the pavement smartly in the joy and delight of his own success and problem-less life.

Another person comes by and we tug at his coat sleeve, but all we get is, "Hey, hey—merry Christmas! How are you?" Once again it's a slap on the back and a quick look at his watch—"Gotta be on my way! Got an appointment!" Or maybe someone *does* stop long enough for us to say that we are hurting and then we watch him become ill at ease and restless because he doesn't know how to deal with pain, and he has to excuse himself on some pretense—but the real reason is that he doesn't want to get involved.

So there we stand on the street corner lonely and more fully convinced than ever that nobody knows the trouble we've seen.

That is what Christmas is all about; there is One who knows. Jesus Christ knows how we feel and how we hurt and how we long to be comforted, sheltered, truly loved—because there is no experience of loneliness or rejection or temptation that He did not know when He was with us. He was made like us in every respect, and in this way He became our great high priest. When we go to Him—as we go to priests—to find help, to have Him speak to God on our behalf, to make prayers for us, never again can we say, "God, you don't understand. We here on earth have struggles you've never gone through as you live in your heavenly peace." Once and for all God in Christ can look at us and say, "I do understand because I too have lived in the flesh with you."

Home for Christmas

JANE MERCHANT

We who would be at home on Christmas day,
Secure in earliest love, with old friends thronging,
Let us remember Mary as she lay
In the strange place begrudging her, faint with longing
For her familiar home in Nazareth,
Where neighbors' talk and her deep silence blended
In little rooms made fragrant by the breath
Of baking, and of small fires carefully tended.

Let us remember men who left behind
Home, family, country, all, because of seeing
One certain light that led them far to find
The Child: and let us be content with being
Away from home, in places far and dim
If only our hearts may be at home with him.

The Gift of Love

DALE EVANS ROGERS

When I was a little girl, the word "Christmas" was magic! It meant climbing into a railroad "sleeping car" and going from our house in Osceola, Arkansas, to my grandfather's home 'way down in Uvalde, Texas.

It meant a happy family reunion with all my aunts and uncles and their children, under the great spreading Texas roof. It meant warm weather in the middle of winter. It meant loads of "goodies" spread on the long family table, with Grandfather at the head thanking God for His abundant blessings and asking that His grace be with us all. It meant a family gathering at an early bedtime around the huge fireplace in Grandfather's bedroom, when we popped corn and ate fresh, luscious fruit and said our good-night prayers. I can still see that blessed room, with the well-thumbed Bible beside my grandfather's big wicker chair. It was quite a family.

But, of course, we were still children then, and we spoke as children, and we understood as children, and it was a long time before we grew enough spiritually to understand Christmas as God meant it to be. (Too many of us, I think, never grow out of our childish concepts of Christmas!)

On Christmas Eve, down there in Texas, we always went to the church first, for the lovely service, and then to the town square with its breathtaking, brilliantly lighted Christmas tree, where there were little gifts for the children. And when we woke up in the morning, there was another Christmas tree which had appeared "miraculously" as we slept; the whole family gathered around it, and again we sensed the spirit of love running through the circle. There were gifts for everyone—but not too much! How grateful I am for that, now! The real gift was the love we had for one another, and the sheer joy of just being together, all one in love.

Is this not the true Christmas? Isn't that what Jesus came to accomplish—"A new commandment I give unto you, That ye love one another . . ."? At least, in those first childhood Christmases, we began to learn that lesson of love. The gifts were secondary; the greatest gift of all was the plain, simple gift of love.

A Christmas Prayer

DOROTHY · HSU

It's Christmas, Lord.
The season to be jolly and all that.
But some of us aren't so jolly.

It's time for families to be together,
To sing "I'll be home for Christmas."
But Lord,
Some of our loved ones won't be home
This year,
Or ever.
And some of us find it very difficult
To shop for Aunt Jane
And Grandpa.
Some of us find our minds so
Occupied with a desperately ill child,
Or a tired worn-out body
That we can't cope with crowds
Or carols.
And some of us find that
Happy memories of Christmases past
Make this Christmas seem
Hollow.
Altogether unbearable.
It's a temptation, Lord,
To just skip it.
To refuse to decorate a tree,
Or send a card.
Or purchase a single present,
For one alone,
Such an approach is possible,
I suppose.
But for little ones in a home,
Lord,
It's unfair.
It takes tremendous strength
For some of us to say
"Merry Christmas" this year.
More strength than
Some of us even possess.
And that's exactly why you came,
Isn't it, Lord?

THE JOY
OF
CHILDREN

It Is Good to Be Children

CHARLES DICKENS

*It is good to be children sometimes,
and never better than at Christmas,
when its mighty Founder was a child
Himself.*

The Wonder of Children

JOAN WINMILL BROWN

Christmas brings out the child in all of us. For brief, beautiful moments we are children again as we see this happy season through the eyes of children. Little fingers touching presents under the tree, ribbons being untied . . . excited voices raised as that special present they have been longing for comes into view.

It is the wonder, the wonder of it all that shines in their eyes.

As we look into these innocent eyes we are reminded of that child that made all of our Christmases possible. The wonder of that first Christmas brings us to Jesus in the manger and in faith we kneel before our Savior in adoration.

The Lamb

WILLIAM BLAKE

Little Lamb, who made thee?
Dost thou know who made thee?
Gave thee life, and bid thee feed,
By the stream and o'er the mead;
Gave thee clothing of delight,
Softest clothing, woolly, bright;
Gave thee such a tender voice,
Making all the vales rejoice?
   Little Lamb, who made thee?
   Dost thou know who made thee?

Little Lamb, I'll tell thee,
Little Lamb, I'll tell thee:
He is callèd by thy name,
For He calls Himself a Lamb.
He is meek, and He is mild;
He became a little child.
I a child, and thou a lamb,
We are callèd by His name.
   Little Lamb, God bless thee!
   Little Lamb, God bless thee!

The Birth That Changed the World

**The story of the very first Christmas
written to be read to little children.**

KENNETH TAYLOR

In those days the Jews were under the rule of the Romans; they had to do whatever the emperor of Rome and his assistants told them to. Now he made a law that the name and address of every Jew must be written down. He instructed everyone to go to the city where his ancestors had lived, so that the Roman officers could record his name. "Ancestors" means relatives who lived hundreds of years before. So Joseph and Mary went to Bethlehem where King David used to live, because they were relatives of his, though he had lived hundreds of years before they were born.

But when they arrived in Bethlehem there was no room for them at the little hotel; it was already full. So they went out to the stable where the donkeys and camels were kept, to sleep in the straw on the floor. And while they were resting in the stable, Mary's baby was born. He was the little son that the angel Gabriel had told her about. Yes, Jesus was born out there in the stable; and Mary dressed Him in some baby clothes she had brought, and wrapped Him up in a blanket, and laid Him in a manger.

That same night some shepherds in the fields outside the town were watching their sheep to protect them from wild animals. Suddenly an angel surrounded by a bright light appeared to them. They were very frightened. But the angel said, "Don't be afraid; for I have good news for you, and for all the world! Tonight, in Bethlehem, your Savior was born! His name is Christ the Lord. And this is how you will know Him: you will find Him wrapped in baby clothes and lying in a manger!"

Then suddenly many, many other angels appeared, praising God and saying, "Glory to God! Peace on earth between God and men!"

After the angels returned to heaven the shepherds said to each other, "Let's hurry to Bethlehem and find the baby!" So they ran into the village and soon found Mary and Joseph, and the baby lying in a manger! Afterward the shepherds returned to their flocks again, praising God for what they had heard and seen.

When the baby was eight days old, His parents named Him Jesus, just as the angel Gabriel had told them to. And they dedicated Him to the Lord, for He was the Son of God.

The Birds' Christmas Tree

CATHERINE MARSHALL

It was Christmas Eve. Outside, the snow was falling in big downy flakes. When we picked up the evening paper from our front steps, we found it almost covered with snow. On the front page was this little notice:

ATTENTION: BIRD LOVERS

This is proving to be a hard winter for the birds in this area to find food. Why not remember the birds too at Christmastime?

I read the notice to Peter John. "I know!" he said excitedly. "Why can't we fix a Christmas tree for the birds?"

Peter-daddy and I agreed that this would be a fine idea.

"Let's put it on the porch of my birdhouse," Peter John said. This was a house he had made in shop at school. It was mounted on a pole in the backyard, and the whole family was proud of it.

We decorated the birds' tree with bits of colored yarn, some tiny popcorn balls, and some cranberries strung together. Then we tied things on the branches that the birds would like: small doughnuts; some empty walnut shells filled with raisins, cracked corn, and sunflower seeds; others filled with peanut butter. We packed some soft suet into pine cones and fastened the cones to the tree.

Then we hid inside the house and watched out of the windows to see what would happen. In no time at all a blue jay, a chickadee, and three sparrows were enjoying a feast. Then came a song sparrow and a pair of redbirds. One of the redbirds stopped eating long enough to sit on top of the birdhouse and sing awhile. Since he was the right Christmas color, we thought he must surely be singing a bird's carol. Anyway, he seemed to be saying in his own way, "Thank you for remembering God's small creatures at Christmastime."

Christmas Past

JOAN WINMILL BROWN

I remember when I was a small child at my grandparents' home, in Wimbledon, England, a ritual that takes me back to their warm, inviting living room. Late Christmas afternoon, when the light was fading quickly outside, my grandfather sat in his favorite chair by the fire and read to me Charles Dickens' *A Christmas Carol.* Curled up by the hearth with a bowl of tangerines and chestnuts—waiting to be roasted—I would be transported back to Victorian England as my grandfather's voice made each word come alive.

The flames leaped in the fireplace, causing the shadows in the room to look like the Ghosts who came to taunt old Ebenezer Scrooge. The old brass-faced clock on the mantelpiece quietly ticked away the time, but I was completely oblivious of the hour.

After Grandfather read the last words, "And so, as Tiny Tim observed, God Bless Us, Every One!" my grandmother would put her head around the door and announce it was time for me to go to bed. The journey upstairs was a spooky one as I hung on to her apron, expecting any minute one of Scrooge's Ghosts to appear. Hastily I would jump into bed, asking Grandmother to make sure there was nothing under it and insisting she tell me a story to help me forget the frightening Dickens' story. Scenes of Father Christmas (Santa Claus), Mother Christmas and the reindeers all resting after such a busy time would be exchanged in my imagination, as Grandmother quietly sat by my bed. Finally, I would fall asleep.

Each Christmas my grandmother would say, "Now don't read that *Christmas Carol* story to Joan, it only scares her," but I would plead to hear it once more. To this day Christmas is not complete without my reading this classic and each time I do I return in memory to my grandparents' fireplace and I once again become, in the remembering, a small, scared and excited little girl.

Tiny Tim—From *A Christmas Carol*

CHARLES DICKENS

Retold by his granddaughter Mary Angela Dickens

It will surprise you all very much to hear that there was once a man who did not like Christmas. In fact, he had been heard on several occasions to use the word *humbug* with regard to it. His name was Scrooge, and he was a hard, sour-tempered man of business, intent only on saving and making money, and caring nothing for anyone. He paid the poor, hardworking clerk in his office as little as he could possibly get the work done for, and lived on as little as possible himself, alone, in two dismal rooms. He was never merry or comfortable, or happy, and he hated other people to be so, and that was the reason why he hated Christmas, because people *will* be happy at Christmas, you know, if they possibly can, and like to have a little money to make themselves and others comfortable.

Well, it was Christmas Eve, a very cold and foggy one, and Mr. Scrooge, having given his poor clerk unwilling permission to spend Christmas Day at home, locked up his office and went home himself in a very bad temper, and with a cold in his head. After having taken some gruel as he sat over a miserable fire in his dismal room, he got into bed, and had some wonderful and disagreeable dreams, to which we will leave him, while we see how Tiny Tim, the son of his poor clerk, spent Christmas Day.

The name of this clerk was Bob Cratchit. He had a wife and five other children besides Tim, who was a weak and delicate little cripple, and for this reason was dearly loved by his father, and the rest of the family; not but what he was a dear little boy too, gentle and patient and loving, with a sweet face of his own, which no one could help looking at.

Whenever he could spare the time, it was Mr. Cratchit's delight to carry his little boy out on his shoulder to see the shops and the people; and today he had taken him to church for the first time.

"Whatever has got your precious father, and your brother Tiny Tim!" exclaimed Mrs. Cratchit. "Here's dinner all ready to be dished up. I've never known him so late on Christmas Day before."

"Here he is, Mother!" cried Belinda, and "Here he is!" cried the other children as Mr. Cratchit came in, his long comforter hanging three feet from under his threadbare coat; for cold as it was, the poor clerk had no topcoat. Tiny Tim was perched on his father's shoulder with his little crutch in his hand.

"And how did Tim behave?" asked Mrs. Cratchit.

"As good as gold and better," replied the father. "I think, wife, the child gets thoughtful, sitting at home so much. He told me, coming home, that he hoped the people in church who saw he was a cripple would be pleased to remember on Christmas Day Who it was who made the lame to walk."

"Bless his sweet heart!" said his mother in a trembling voice, and the father's voice trembled too, as he remarked that Tiny Tim was growing strong and hearty at last.

Dinner was waiting to be dished up. Mrs. Cratchit proudly placed a goose upon the table. Belinda brought in the apple sauce, and Peter the mashed potatoes; the other children set chairs, Tim's as usual, close to his father's; and Tim was so excited that he rapped the table with his knife, and cried "Hurrah!" After the goose came the pudding, with a great smell of steam, like washing day, as it came out of the copper; in it came, all ablaze, with its sprig of holly in the middle, and was eaten to the last morsel. Then apples and oranges were set upon the table, and a shovelful of chestnuts on the fire, and Mr. Cratchit served round some hot sweet stuff out of a jug as they closed round the fire, and said, "A Merry Christmas to us all, my dears. God bless us!" "God bless us every one!" echoed Tiny Tim, and then they drank each other's health, and Mr. Scrooge's health, and told stories and sang songs—Tim, who had a sweet little voice, singing, very well indeed, a song about a child who was lost in the snow on Christmas Day.

Now I told you that Mr. Scrooge had some disagreeable and wonderful dreams on Christmas Eve, and so he had; and in one of them he dreamt that a Christmas spirit showed him his clerk's home; he saw them all gathered round the fire, and heard them drink his health, and Tiny Tim's song, and he took special note of Tiny Tim himself.

In his dreams that night Scrooge visited all sorts of places and saw all sorts of people, for different spirits came to him and led him about where they would, and presently he was taken again to his poor clerk's home. The mother was doing some needlework, seated by the table; a tear dropped on it now and then, and she said, poor thing, that the work, which was black, hurt her eyes. The children sat, sad and silent, about the room, except Tiny Tim, who was not there. Upstairs the father, with his face hidden in his hands, sat beside a little bed, on which lay a tiny figure, white and still. "My little child, my pretty little child," he sobbed, as the tears fell through his fingers onto the floor. "Tiny Tim died because his father was too poor to give him what was necessary to make him well; *you* kept him poor," said the dream spirit to Mr. Scrooge. The father kissed the cold, little face on the bed, and went downstairs, where the sprays of holly still remained about the humble room; and, taking his hat, went out, with a wistful glance at the little crutch in the corner as he shut the door. Mr. Scrooge saw all this, and many more things as strange and sad—the spirit took care of that; but, wonderful to relate, he woke next morning feeling a different man— feeling as he had never felt in his life before.

"Why, I am as light as a feather, and as happy as an angel, and as merry as a schoolboy," he said to himself. "A Merry Christmas to everybody! A happy New Year to all the world." And a few minutes later he was ordering a turkey to be taken round to Tiny Tim's house, a turkey so large that the man who took it had to go in a cab.

Next morning poor Bob Cratchit crept into the office a few minutes late, expecting to be roundly abused and scolded for it; he soon found, however, that his master was a very different man to the one who had grudged him his Christmas holiday, for there was Scrooge telling him heartily he was going to raise his salary and asking quite affectionately after Tiny Tim! "And mind you make up a good fire in your room before you set to work, Bob," he said, as he closed his own door.

Bob could hardly believe his eyes and ears, but it was all true, and more prosperous times came to his family, and happier, for Tiny Tim did not die—not a bit of it. Mr. Scrooge was a second father to him from that day; he wanted for nothing, and grew up strong and hearty. Mr. Scrooge loved him, and well he might, for was it not Tiny Tim who had unconsciously, through the Christmas dream spirit, touched his hard heart, and caused him to be a good and happy man.

Ah, Lord, Who Hast Created All

MARTIN LUTHER

Ah, Lord, who hast created all,
How hast Thou made Thee weak and small,
That Thou must choose Thy infant bed
Where ass and ox but lately fed?

Mr. Edwards Meets Santa Claus

LAURA INGALLS WILDER

. . . Santa Claus said: "I understand you're living now down along the Verdigris River. Have you ever met up, down yonder, with two little young girls named Mary and Laura?"

"I surely am acquainted with them," Mr. Edwards replied.

"It rests heavy on my mind," said Santa Claus. "They are both of them sweet, pretty, good little young things, and I know they are expecting me. I surely do hate to disappoint two good little girls like them. Yet with the water up the way it is, I can't ever make it across that creek. I can figure no way whatsoever to get to their cabin this year. Edwards," Santa Claus said, "would you do me the favor to fetch them their gifts one time?"

"I'll do that, and with pleasure," Mr. Edwards told him.

Then Santa Claus and Mr. Edwards stepped across the street to the hitching posts where the pack-mule was tied. ("Didn't he have his reindeer?" Laura asked. "You know he couldn't," Mary said. "There isn't any snow." Exactly, said Mr. Edwards. Santa Claus traveled with a pack-mule in the Southwest.)

And Santa Claus uncinched the pack and looked through it, and he took out the presents for Mary and Laura.

"Oh, what are they?" Laura cried; but Mary asked, "Then what did he do?"

Then he shook hands with Mr. Edwards, and he swung up on his fine bay horse. Santa Claus rode well, for a man of his weight and build. And he tucked his long white whiskers under his bandanna. "So long, Edwards," he said, and he rode away on the Fort Dodge trail, leading his pack-mule and whistling.

Laura and Mary were silent an instant, thinking of that.

Then Ma said, "You may look now, girls."

Something was shining bright in the top of Laura's stocking. She squealed and jumped out of bed. So did Mary, but Laura beat her to the fireplace. And the shining thing was a glittering new tin cup.

Mary had one exactly like it.

These new tin cups were their very own. Now they each had a cup to drink out of. Laura jumped up and down and shouted and laughed, but Mary stood still and looked with shining eyes at her own tin cup.

Then they plunged their hands into the stockings again. And they pulled out two long, long sticks of candy. It was peppermint candy, striped red and white. They looked and looked at that beautiful candy, and Laura licked her stick, just one lick. But Mary was not so greedy. She didn't take even one lick of her stick.

Those stockings weren't empty yet. Mary and Laura pulled out two small packages. They unwrapped them, and each found a little heart-shaped cake. Over their delicate brown tops was sprinkled white sugar. The sparkling grains lay like tiny drifts of snow.

The cakes were too pretty to eat. Mary and Laura just looked at them. But at last Laura turned hers over, and she nibbled a tiny nibble from underneath, where it wouldn't show. And the inside of that little cake was white!

It had been made of pure white flour, and sweetened with white sugar.

Laura and Mary never would have looked in their stockings again. The cups and the cakes and the candy were almost too much. They were too happy to speak. But Ma asked if they were sure the stockings were empty.

Then they put their arms down inside them, to make sure.

And in the very toe of each stocking was a shining bright, new penny!

They had never even thought of such a thing as having a penny. Think of having a whole penny for your very own. Think of having a cup and a cake and a stick of candy *and* a penny.

There never had been such a Christmas.

Now of course, right away, Laura and Mary should have thanked Mr. Edwards for bringing those lovely presents all the way from Independence. But they had forgotten all about Mr. Edwards. They had even forgotten Santa Claus. In a minute they would have remembered, but before they did, Ma said gently, "Aren't you going to thank Mr. Edwards?"

"Oh, thank you, Mr. Edwards! Thank you!" they said, and they meant it with all their hearts. Pa shook Mr. Edwards' hand, too, and shook it again. Pa and Ma and Mr. Edwards acted as if they were almost crying, Laura didn't know why. So she gazed again at her beautiful presents.

She looked up again when Ma gasped. And Mr. Edwards was taking sweet potatoes out of his pockets. He said they had helped to balance the package on his head when he swam across the creek. He thought Pa and Ma might like them, with the Christmas turkey.

There were nine sweet potatoes. Mr. Edwards had brought them all the way from town, too. It was just too much. Pa said so. "It's too much, Edwards," he said. They never could thank him enough.

Mary and Laura were too much excited to eat breakfast. They drank the milk from their shining new cups, but they could not swallow the rabbit stew and the cornmeal mush.

"Don't make them, Charles," Ma said. "It will soon be dinnertime."

For Christmas dinner there was the tender, juicy, roasted turkey. There were the sweet potatoes, baked in the ashes and carefully wiped so that you could eat the good skins, too. There was a loaf of salt-rising bread made from the last of the white flour.

And after all that there were stewed dried blackberries and little cakes. But these little cakes were made with brown sugar and they did not have white sugar sprinkled over their tops.

Then Pa and Ma and Mr. Edwards sat by the fire and talked about Christmas times back in Tennessee and up north in the Big Woods. But Mary and Laura looked at their beautiful cakes and played with their pennies and drank water out of their new cups. And little by little they licked and sucked their sticks of candy, till each stick was sharp-pointed on one end.

That was a happy Christmas.

A Christmas Smile
The Muffin Family

GIL BEERS

"Yuk! Look at all those weird things Mini wants for Christmas," Maxi grumbled in the toy store. Mommi had given him part of Mini's Christmas *want list*, the part Mommi said he could afford.

"Now to find all these things and see how much each one costs," Maxi said.

The first item was in the doll section. "A Baby Bunnikins diaper tote bag," Maxi read to the clerk, turning a little pink and looking the other way as he did.

"That is four dollars and ninety-five cents plus tax," said the clerk.

Maxi frowned. He thought of the things he could buy for himself for $4.95. *I could get a Star Fighter game or a cowboy hat on sale, or five chocolate sundaes.*

The next item on Mini's list was in the dollhouse section. "Floor lamp for dollhouse," Maxi read to the clerk.

"That's three dollars and ninety-five cents plus tax," said the clerk.

I could buy a lot of things for that! Like a checker set, or model airplane, or four chocolate sundaes, Maxi thought with a frown.

"Let's try another one on the list," Maxi mumbled to himself. "How about this cookie cutter set?"

"That will be two dollars and ninety-five cents plus tax," the clerk said.

Maxi almost bought that one, but he frowned again when he thought of all the things he could buy for himself for $2.95. *I could get that big bag of marbles I saw over there, or some dominoes, or three chocolate sundaes*, he thought.

He looked again at Mini's list. "How much is this plastic picture frame?" he asked the clerk.

"One dollar and ninety-five cents plus tax," said the clerk.

Maxi reached into his pocket for the money, but then he frowned again as he thought of the things he could buy for himself for $1.95. He had to think longer this time, but finally he thought of a scorecard packet for his baseball game, or two chocolate sundaes.

What was next on Mini's list? "Note pads," Maxi read. "That can't cost much."

"That's ninety-five cents plus tax," said the clerk.

Maxi took a dollar from his pocket and almost gave it to the clerk. But it looked bigger than any dollar he had ever seen.

"That's a *whole dollar*," Maxi said with a frown. "I could buy a . . . well, uh . . . I could buy a chocolate sundae for that!"

Suddenly a chocolate sundae seemed like the most important thing in the world. Maxi ran to Pop's Sweet Shop.

While Maxi waited for Pop to finish another order, he thought about his Christmas shopping. And he thought about when the Muffins would open their gifts at Christmas.

Maxi could see Mini's happy face and hear her delighted squeals when she opened her gifts. Then Maxi suddenly realized that Mini would not squeal with delight when she opened his gift. He had not bought one!

Maxi imagined Mini's sad face. Then he frowned his biggest frown yet.

He remembered a Bible verse he learned in Sunday school. It said, "God loves a cheerful giver" (2 Corinthians 9:7).

Maxi realized he hadn't passed by each gift because of what it would cost but because he was an uncheerful giver. In fact, he wasn't a giver at all!

From *Little Grey Rabbit's Christmas*

ALISON UTTLEY

"Grey Rabbit! He's been! Wake up! He's been in the night!"

"Who?" cried Grey Rabbit, rubbing her eyes and sitting up in a fright. "Who? Has Rat been?"

"Santa Claus!" cried Hare, capering up and down by her bed. "Be quick and come downstairs and see the surprises."

Grey Rabbit dressed hurriedly, but there was a little twinkle in her eyes as she entered the room.

"Look what he brought me!" cried Squirrel, holding out a pair of fur mittens and bedroom slippers made from sheep's wool.

"And he gave me a spotted handkerchief, and a musical box," cried Hare excitedly, and he turned the handle of the little round box from which came a jolly tune which set their feet dancing.

"Look at the Kissing Bunch!" Hare went on. "Isn't it lovely! Let's all kiss under it."

So they gave their Christmas morning kisses under the round Christmas Bunch in the time-honored way.

Christmas Day: Postscripts by Ilbereth

J. R. R. TOLKIEN

J. R. R. Tolkien, author of *The Lord of the Rings, The Hobbit,* etc., and Professor of English Language and Literature at Oxford, England, used to write letters filled with imagination and humor from Father Christmas (Santa Claus) to his children each year. They not only looked forward to receiving their gifts, but also to a communication from the North Pole. The four children would find the letters in the house after Father Christmas' visit, or sometimes the postman brought them.

Each year they learned more of Father Christmas' house, his reindeer, Snow-elves, Red Gnomes, Snow men, Cave-bears, the North Polar Bear and his nephews. The Polar Bear was the chief assistant, but eventually Father Christmas employed an Elf named Ilbereth as his secretary. This Elf helped arm the house against an attack of Goblins, and later wrote the following poem about Polar Bear!

Now Christmas day has come round again—
and poor Polar Bear has got a bad pain!
They say he's swallowed a couple of pounds
of nuts without cracking the shells! It sounds
a Polarish sort of thing to do—
but that isn't all, between me and you:
he's eaten a ton of various goods
and recklessly mixed all his favorite foods,
honey with ham, and turkey and treacle,
and pickles with milk. I think that a week'll
be needed to put the old bear on his feet.
And I mustn't forget his particular treat:
plum pudding with sausages and turkish delight
covered with cream and devoured at a bite!
And after this dish, he stood on his head—
it's rather a wonder the poor fellow's not dead!

And here is Polar Bear's reply:

> *Absolute rot:*
> *I have not got*
> *A pain in my pot.*
> *I do not eat*
> *Turkey or meat:*
> *I stick to the sweet.*
> *Which is why*
> *(As all know) I*
> *Am so sweet myself*
> *You thinnuous elf!*
> *Goodby!*

A Visit from St. Nicholas

CLEMENT CLARKE MOORE

A caretaker at the New York home of Clement Clarke Moore was one of the sources of inspiration for the jovial, rotund, jolly, bewhiskered St. Nicholas in this famous and beloved poem.

Moore, a dignified professor of theology, who published sermons and classical verse, at first did not wish to claim authorship. The poem was written for his children, and he first recited it to them and a few guests on December 23, 1822. One guest requested a copy and the following year sent it anonymously to the Troy *Sentinel*, in Troy, New York. It was then published on the anniversary of its first reading. A note by the editor read: "We know not to whom we are indebted for the description of that unwearied patron of children, but from whomever it may have come, we give thanks for it."

In 1844 Moore finally admitted authorship and the world could acknowledge the one who had brought it such delight.

'Twas the night before Christmas, when all through the house
Not a creature was stirring, not even a mouse;
The stockings were hung by the chimney with care,
In hopes that St. Nicholas soon would be there;
The children were nestled all snug in their beds,
While visions of sugarplums danced in their heads;
And mamma in her kerchief and I in my cap
Had just settled our brains for a long winter's nap,
When out on the lawn there arose such a clatter,
I sprang from my bed to see what was the matter.
Away to the window I flew like a flash,
Tore open the shutters, and threw up the sash;
The moon, on the breast of the new-fallen snow,
Gave a luster of midday to objects below;
When what to my wondering eyes should appear
But a miniature sleigh and eight tiny reindeer,
With a little old driver, so lively and quick,
I knew in a moment, it must be St. Nick.
More rapid than eagles his coursers they came,
And he whistled and shouted and called them by name:
"Now Dasher! now Dancer! now Prancer! now Vixen!

On, Comet! on, Cupid! on, Donner and Blitzen!
To the top of the porch! To the top of the wall!
Now, dash away, dash away, dash away, all!"
As dry leaves that before the wild hurricane fly,
When they meet with an obstacle, mount to the sky,
So up to the housetop the coursers they flew,
With the sleigh full of toys and St. Nicholas too.
And then, in a twinkling, I heard on the roof
The prancing and pawing of each little hoof.
As I drew in my head and was turning around,
Down the chimney St. Nicholas came with a bound.
He was dressed all in fur, from his head to his foot,
And his clothes were all tarnished with ashes and soot;
A bundle of toys he had flung on his back,
And he looked like a peddler just opening his pack.
His eyes: how they twinkled! his dimples: how merry!
His cheeks were like roses, his nose like a cherry;
His droll little mouth was drawn up like a bow,
And the beard on his chin was as white as the snow.
The stump of a pipe he held tight in his teeth,
And the smoke, it encircled his head like a wreath:
He had a broad face, and a little round belly,
That shook, when he laughed, like a bowl full of jelly;
He was chubby and plump, a right jolly old elf;
And I laughed, when I saw him, in spite of myself,
A wink of his eye and a twist of his head
Soon gave me to know I had nothing to dread.
He spoke not a word, but went straight to his work,
And filled all the stockings; then turned with a jerk,
And laying his finger aside of his nose,
And giving a nod, up the chimney he rose.
He sprang to his sleigh, to his team gave a whistle,
And away they all flew like the down of a thistle;
But I heard him exclaim, ere he drove out of sight,
"Happy Christmas to all, and to all a good night!"

Yes, Virginia, There Is a Santa Claus

The New York Sun

Little Virginia O'Hanlon was very upset when she was told by her friends that there was no such thing as Santa Claus. When she asked her father, he did not want to give her a straight answer. Remembering that he always wrote to the New York *Sun* for advice about any question that came up in the family regarding how to pronounce a word, or a historical fact, Virginia decided to write a letter to the editor.

Her letter and the consequent reply have been cherished down through the years:

The New York *Sun*, September 21, 1897

We take pleasure in answering at once and thus prominently the communication below, expressing at the same time our great gratification that its faithful author is numbered among the friends of *The Sun:*

Dear Editor:
I am 8 years old.
Some of my little friends say there is no Santa Claus.
Papa says "If you see it in *The Sun* it's so."
Please tell me the truth, is there a Santa Claus?

Virginia O'Hanlon
115 West 95th Street

Virginia, your little friends are wrong. They have been affected by the skepticism of a skeptical age. They do not believe except what they see. They think that nothing can be which is not comprehensible by their little minds. All minds, Virginia, whether they be men's or children's, are little. In this great universe of ours man is a mere insect, an ant, in his intellect, as compared with the boundless world about him, as measured by the intelligence capable of grasping the whole of truth and knowledge.

Yes, Virginia, there is a Santa Claus. He exists as certainly as love and generosity and devotion exist, and you know that they abound and give to your life its highest beauty and joy. Alas! how dreary would be the world if there were no Santa Claus! It would be as dreary as if there were no Virginias. There would be no childlike faith then, no poetry, no romance to make tolerable this existence. We should have no enjoyment, except in sense and sight. The eternal light with which childhood fills the world would be extinguished.

Not believe in Santa Claus! You might as well not believe in fairies! You might get your papa to hire men to watch in all the chimneys on Christmas Eve to catch Santa Claus, but even if they did not see Santa Claus coming down, what would that prove? Nobody sees Santa Claus, but that is no sign that there is no Santa Claus. The most real things in the world are those that neither children nor men can see. Did you ever see fairies dancing on the lawn? Of course not, but that's no proof that they are not there. Nobody can conceive or imagine all the wonders there are unseen and unseeable in the world.

You tear apart the baby's rattle and see what makes the noise inside, but there is a veil covering the unseen world which not the strongest man, nor even the united strength of all the strongest men that ever lived, could tear apart. Only faith, fancy, poetry, love, romance, can push aside that curtain and view and picture the supernal beauty and glory beyond. Is it all real? Ah, Virginia, in all this world there is nothing else real and abiding.

No Santa Claus! Thank God he lives, and he lives forever. A thousand years from now, Virginia, nay, ten times ten thousand years from now, he will continue to make glad the heart of childhood.

Paddington's Christmas

From *More About Paddington*

MICHAEL BOND

. . . When he made his way up to bed later that evening, his mind was in such a whirl, and he was so full of good things, he could hardly climb the stairs—let alone think about anything. He wasn't quite sure which he had enjoyed most. The presents, the Christmas dinner, the games or the tea—with the special marmalade-layer birthday cake Mrs. Bird had made in his honor. Pausing on the corner halfway up, he decided he had enjoyed giving his own presents best of all.

"Paddington! Whatever have you got there?" He jumped and hastily hid his paw behind his back as he heard Mrs. Bird calling from the bottom of the stairs.

"It's only some sixpence pudding, Mrs. Bird," he called, looking over the banisters guiltily. "I thought I might get hungry during the night and I didn't want to take any chances."

"Honestly!" Mrs. Bird exclaimed, as she was joined by the others. "What *does* that bear look like? A paper hat about ten sizes too big on his head—Mr. Gruber's scrapbook in one paw—and a plate of Christmas pudding in the other!"

"I don't care what he looks like," said Mrs. Brown, "so long as he stays that way. The place wouldn't be the same without him."

But Paddington was too far away to hear what was being said. He was already sitting up in bed, busily writing in his scrapbook.

First of all, there was a very important notice to go on the front page. It said:

PADINGTUN BROWN,
32 WINDSOR GARDENS,
LUNDUN
ENGLAND
YUROPE,
THE WORLD

Then, on the next page he added, in large capital letters: MY ADD-VENTURES. CHAPTER WUN.

Paddington sucked his pen thoughtfully for a moment and then carefully replaced the top on the bottle of ink before it had a chance to fall over on the sheets. He felt much too sleepy to write any more. But he didn't really mind. Tomorrow was another day—and he felt quite sure he *would* have some more adventures—even if he didn't know what they were going to be as yet.

Paddington lay back and pulled the blankets up round his whiskers. It was warm and comfortable and he sighed contentedly as he closed his eyes. It was nice being a bear. Especially a bear called Paddington.

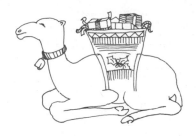

Simpkin's Christmas

From *The Tailor of Gloucester*

BEATRIX POTTER

The tailor lay ill for three days and nights; and then it was Christmas Eve, and very late at night. The moon climbed up over the roofs and chimneys, and looked over the gateway into College Court. There were no lights in the windows, nor any sound in the houses; all the city of Gloucester was fast asleep under the snow.

And still Simpkin wanted his mice, and mewed as he stood beside the four-post bed.

But it is the old story that all the beasts can talk in the night between Chritmas Eve and Christmas Day in the morning (though there are very few folk that can hear them, or know what it is that they say).

When the Cathedral clock struck twelve there was an answer—like an echo of the chimes—and Simpkin heard it, and came out of the tailor's door, and wandered about in the snow.

From all the roofs and gables and old wooden houses in Gloucester came a thousand merry voices singing the old Christmas rhymes—all the old songs that ever I heard of, and some that I didn't know, like Whittington's bells.

First and loudest the cocks cried out—"Dame, get up, and bake your pies!"

"Oh, dilly, dilly, dilly!" sighed Simpkin.

And now in a garret there were lights and sounds of dancing, and cats came from over the way.

"Hey, diddle, diddle, the cat and the fiddle! All the cats in Gloucester —except me," said Simpkin.

Under the wooden eaves the starlings and sparrows sang of Christmas pies; the jackdaws woke up in the Cathedral tower; and although it was the middle of the night the throstles and robins sang; the air was quite full of little twittering tunes.

But it was all rather provoking to poor hungry Simpkin!

Particularly he was vexed with some little shrill voices from behind a wooden lattice. I think that there were bats, because they always have very small voices—especially in a black forest, when they talk in their sleep, like the Tailor of Gloucester.

An Alphabet of Christmas

Author unknown

A   is for Animals who shared the stable.
B   for the Babe with their manger for cradle.
C   for the Carols so blithe and so gay.
D   for December, the twenty-fifth day.
E   for the Eve when we're all so excited.
F   for the Fun when the tree's at last lighted.
G   is the Goose which you all know is fat.
H   is the Holly you stick in your hat.
I   for the Ivy that clings to the wall.
J   is for Jesus, the cause of it all.
K   for the Kindness begot by this feast.
L   is the Light shining way in the east.
M   for the Mistletoe, all green and white.
N   for the Nowells we sing Christmas night.
O   for the Oxen, the first to adore Him.
P   for the Presents Wise Men laid before Him.
Q   for the Queerness that this should have been
     Near two thousand years before you were seen.
R   for the Reindeer leaping the roofs.
S   for the Stockings that Santa Claus stuffs.
T   for the Toys, the Tinsel, the Tree.
U   is for Us—the whole family.
V   is for Visitors bringing us cheer.
W   is Welcome to the happy New Year.
X   Y Z bother me! All I can say,
     Is this is the end of my Christmas lay.
     So now to you all, wherever you be,
     A merry, merry Christmas, and many may you see!

THE JOY OF CHRISTMAS FARE

Joyful Hospitality

JOAN WINMILL BROWN

From the heart of the house comes the joy of hospitality and Christmas fare. The kitchen becomes a gathering place as the days approach this special day. The sounds, the aromas of the season begin here. The joyful anticipation of the family gathering around the Christmas table—friends dropping in, parties being given—all this is a bond with the past as so many dishes that have been handed down from generation to generation are selected and baked.

Christmas is a time of welcoming. Looking back into the Old Testament, Abraham entertained three celestial visitors. He saw that they had water, bread, cakes of fine meal, dressed calf, butter and milk and "he stood by them under the tree, and they did eat" (Genesis 18:8).

Paul tells us, "Be not forgetful to entertain strangers: for thereby some have entertained angels unawares" (Hebrews 13:2).

Welcoming strangers was a custom in the early history of England. In the great halls of the palaces and stately homes, open house was the dominant note of the Christmas feast. Family gatherings were not complete without the visits of some strangers, whether they were poor or distinguished.

Cookies are an integral part of Christmas. The house takes on the excitement of the season as soon as the first batch of cookies is baked and the delicious aroma permeates the house. Countries around the world have their favorite recipes, which have been lovingly handed down from mother to daughter over the years.

It is from the Dutch that we receive our word *cookie*. Their word *koekje* has become part of the American language.

These cookies from Holland are particularly tempting and are very easy to make.

Jan Hagel Cookies
(Hollanders)

1 cup sugar	*1 egg (beaten lightly)*
2 cups sifted flour	*½ cup chopped pecans*
1 cup butter	

Preheat oven to 350° F. Cream room-temperature butter and sugar together and then gradually add the flour. Press mixture ½″ thick into two ungreased pans 13″ × 8½″ or one 15½″ × 10½″ pan. Brush beaten egg over top and sprinkle with the nuts. Bake until golden—15–25 minutes. These cookies burn easily so be careful to watch last few minutes of baking time. Cool until they look set, and then cut into squares or diamonds.

Before the custom of gift-giving began, children in Germany would leave their plates on the kitchen table on Christmas Eve. In the morning they would find perhaps an orange, nuts, candies and a delicious supply of one of the smallest cookies—peppernuts. There are many variations as to what is added—dates, raisins, citron, lemon, nuts or coconut—but this is the basic recipe.

Pfeffernüsse
(German Peppernuts)

1 cup dark syrup
1 cup sour cream
1 teaspoon soda
Flour (approximately 5 cups)

⅓ to ½ cup anise seeds
1 cup margarine
1½ cups sugar
1 teaspoon salt

Mix all together and chill. Roll dough to ½" and cut into pieces the size of a hazelnut. Bake as needed at 350° F. for approximately 10 minutes or until brown. (The dough can first be kept in the refrigerator to "ripen" for several days. This enhances the flavor.)

Now Christmas Comes

Virginia Almanack
1766

Now Christmas comes, 'tis fit that we
Should feast and sing, and merry be:
Keep open house, let fiddlers play,
A fig for cold, sing care away . . .

Christmas Pudding

2 cups flour
2 level teaspoons baking powder
¼ teaspoon each, ground cloves
   and cinnamon
½ teaspoon each, mace and salt
1 cup flour
½ pound beef suet

½ pound raisins
½ pound currants
2 ounces citron, cut fine
1 cup sugar
Grated rind of 1 lemon
2 eggs
½ cup milk

Sift together, three times, the two-cup flour, baking powder, spices and salt. Chop fine the suet, mixing it with the one cup of flour; add the fruit, sugar, lemon rind, and the flour mixture together. Mix this thoroughly, then stir in the eggs beaten very light and mixed with the milk. The mixture should be quite stiff. Steam on low heat six hours in a buttered two-quart mold, in a kettle of water on rack. Serve with hard sauce or custard.

Christmas in the Olden Times

SIR WALTER SCOTT

. . . *Garnished with ribbons, blithely trowls*
There the huge sirloin reeked: Hard by
Plum-porridge stood, and Christmas pye;
Nor failed Old Scotland to produce
At such high-tide, her savory goose . . .

The mention of roast goose conjures up in our minds that favorite dish of Dickensian times. Before the introduction of the turkey to Europe, this succulent bird reigned king of the Victorian festive table. (A traditional stuffing in Hungary, Germany, Belgium, Holland and Yugoslavia is made with prunes and apples.)

Roast Goose

Preheat oven to 325° F. Prepare bird for roasting in the same way as turkey. Also rub inside well with half a lemon before stuffing. Prick skin well all over with a sharp fork so fat underneath will drain off during cooking. Rub skin well with salt (this helps to crispen skin). Place bird breast side up on a rack in a shallow roasting pan and roast uncovered, draining off drippings as they accumulate and pricking as needed. *Note:* For a particularly crisp skin, raise oven temperature to 450° F. during last ½ hour of roasting. Also drain all drippings from pan and spoon ¼–½ cup ice water over bird.

Roasting times with oven temperature of 325° F.

4–6 pounds	2¾–3 hours
6–8 pounds	3–3½ hours
8–12 pounds	3½–4½ hours
12–14 pounds	4½–5 hours

From *A Christmas Carol*

CHARLES DICKENS

. . . Such a bustle ensued that you might have thought a goose the rarest of all birds; a feathered phenomenon, to which a black swan was a matter of course—and in truth it was something very like it in that house. Mrs. Cratchit made the gravy (ready beforehand in a little saucepan) hissing hot; Master Peter mashed the potatoes with incredible vigor; Miss Belinda sweetened up the apple sauce; Martha dusted the hot plates; Bob took Tiny Tim beside him in a tiny corner at the table; the two young Cratchits set chairs for everybody, not forgetting themselves, and mounting guard upon their posts, crammed spoons into their mouths, lest they should shriek for goose before their turn came to be helped. At last the dishes were set on, and grace was said. It was succeeded by a breathless pause, as Mrs. Cratchit, looking slowly all along the carving knife, prepared to plunge it in the breast; but when she did, and when the long-expected gush of stuffing issued forth, one murmur of delight arose all round the board, and even Tiny Tim, excited by the two young Cratchits, beat on the table with the handle of his knife, and feebly cried Hurrah!

There never was such a goose. Bob said he didn't believe there ever was such a goose cooked. Its tenderness and flavor, size and cheapness, were the themes of universal admiration. Eked out by apple sauce and mashed potatoes, it was a sufficient dinner for the whole family; indeed, as Mrs. Cratchit said with great delight (surveying one small atom of a bone upon the dish), they hadn't ate it all at last! Yet every one had had enough, and the youngest Cratchits in particular were steeped in sage and onion to the eyebrows! But now the plates were changed by Miss Belinda, Mrs. Cratchit left the room alone—too nervous to bear witnesses—to take the pudding up, and bring it in.

Suppose it should not be done enough! Suppose it should break in turning out! Suppose somebody should have got over the wall of the backyard, and stolen it, while they were merry with the goose—a supposition at which the two young Cratchits became livid! All sorts of horrors were supposed.

Hallo! A great deal of steam! The pudding was out of the copper. A smell like a washing day! That was the cloth. A smell like an eating house and a pastry cook's next door to each other, with a laundress's next door to that! That was the pudding! In half a minute Mrs. Cratchit entered—flushed, but smiling proudly—with the pudding, like a speckled cannon ball, so hard and firm, blazing in half of half a quartern of ignited brandy, and bedight with Christmas holly stuck into the top.

Oh, a wonderful pudding! Bob Cratchit said, and calmly, too, that he regarded it as the greatest success achieved by Mrs. Cratchit since their marriage. Mrs. Cratchit said that, now the weight was off her mind, she would confess she had her doubts about the quantity of flour. Everybody had something to say about it, but nobody said or thought it was at all a small pudding for a large family. It would have been flat heresy to do so. Any Cratchit would have blushed to hint at such a thing.

At last the dinner was all done, the cloth was cleared, the hearth swept, and the fire made up. The compound in the jug being tasted, and considered perfect, apples and oranges were put upon the table, and a shovelful of chestnuts on the fire. Then all the Cratchit family drew round the hearth, in what Bob Cratchit called a circle, meaning half a one; and at Bob Cratchit's elbow stood the family display of glass. Two tumblers and a custard cup without a handle.

These held the hot stuff from the jug, however, as well as golden goblets would have done; and Bob served it out with beaming looks, while the chestnuts on the fire sputtered and cracked noisily. Then Bob proposed: "A Merry Christmas to us all, my dears. God bless us!" Which all the family re-echoed.

"God bless us every one!" said Tiny Tim, the last of all . . .

Christmas Is Come

Virginia Almanack
Eighteenth Century

Christmas is come, hang on the pot,
Let spits turn round, and ovens be hot;
Beef, pork, and poultry, now provide
To feast thy neighbors at this tide . . .

Christmas in Williamsburg

JOAN WINMILL BROWN

In Williamsburg, Virginia, the eighteenth century brought food of incredible succulence to the tables of the citizens. On Christmas Day, after a service at the Bruton Parish Church, families and their friends would return home either on foot, on horse or by carriage, through the snow, to enjoy an enormous feast.

A typical menu would include roast turkey with grapes, glazed ham, spiced crab apples, asparagus, broccoli, and glazed sweet potato slices. For dessert the ladened table would hold Christmas pudding, hard sauce, Williamsburg fruitcake, mince, pecan, and cherry pies and—to finish—a dazzling dish of candied orange and lemon peel, cherries, marzipan, and crystallized ginger.

All this would have been served on a beautifully decorated table; the centerpiece probably consisting of leaves from the spruce or fir tree, adorned with fruits, berries and nuts. The mellow candlelight shed a warm glow and lit up the faces of those seated around the festive table. As they partook of this bountiful meal, for a while the penetrating cold outside would be forgotten, as each heart was warmed with the joy of good food and fellowship.

During the Christmas season, children in some homes in New England have a small buffet set up for them and it is fun to see the enjoyment this brings. A table, covered with an antique quilt, is decorated with small baskets containing old toys, gingerbread boys, Christmas cookies, and pitchers of apple cider. There are baskets, too, filled with inexpensive gifts for each child.

Preparations can be shared with the children, and the beginning of traditions in the kitchen can start as they help to make—

Gingerbread Boys

2½ cups sifted flour
½ teaspon salt
2 teaspoons ginger
½ cup butter or margarine

½ cup sugar
½ cup molasses
½ teaspoon baking soda
¼ cup hot water

DECORATIONS
Cinnamon candies ("red-hots")
Seedless raisins

EASY ICING

1 cup sifted confectioners' sugar
¼ teaspoon salt

½ teaspoon vanilla
1 tablespoon (about) heavy cream

Sift flour with salt and ginger and set aside. Melt butter in a large saucepan over low heat, remove from heat and mix in sugar, then molasses. Dissolve soda in hot water. Add dry ingredients to molasses mixture alternately with soda-water, beginning and ending with dry ingredients. Chill dough 2–3 hours. Preheat oven to 350° F. Roll out dough, a small portion at a time, ⅛″ thick. Cut with gingerbread boy cutter, handling dough carefully, and transfer cookies to ungreased baking sheets (they should be spaced about 2″ apart). Press on cinnamon candies for buttons and raisins for eyes and bake 10–12 minutes until lightly browned. Cool 2–3 minutes on sheets, then lift to wire racks. While cookies cool, prepare icing: mix sugar, salt, and vanilla; add cream, a few drops at a time, mixing well after each addition until icing is smooth and will hold a shape. Using a decorating tube, pipe outlines for collars, boots, cuffs, and belts. If you like, make a little extra icing, tint yellow, and use to pipe in hair. When frosting has hardened, store airtight. *Note:* Gingerbread boys can be made several days ahead and piped with icing shortly before serving. If they soften in storage, warm 3–5 minutes at 350° F. to crispen, then cool on racks. About 130 calories each. Makes two dozen.

*And may your happiness ever spread
Like butter on hot gingerbread.*

Old Couplet

Christmas Day Menu at the White House

circa 1887

BREAKFAST

Boiled Rice
Broiled Salt Mackerel
Poached Eggs à la Creme
Potato Fillets
Feather Griddle Cakes
Wheat Bread
Coffee

DINNER

Oysters on Half Shell
Game Soup
Boiled Whitefish   Sauce Maître d'Hôtel
Roast Goose   Apple Sauce
Boiled Potatoes
Mashed Turnips
Creamed Parsnips
Stewed Onions
Boiled Rice
Lobster Salad
Canvasback Duck
Christmas Plum Pudding   Sauce
Vanilla Ice Cream
Mince Pie   Orange Jelly
Delicate Cake
Salted Almonds
Confectionery Fruits
Coffee

SUPPER

Cold Roast Goose
Oyster Patties
Cold Slaw

Charlotte Russe
Peach Jelly
Tea

From *The White House Cook Book*, 1887
(Hugo Zieman—Steward of the White
House—and Mrs. F. L. Gillette)

The hospitality of the White House is renowned throughout the world. "Par excellence" describes the cuisine. Each President and his wife brought their own personal touches during their administration.

Here is a Christmas menu made up of some of the Presidents and their wives' favorite dishes. (Many have been modernized.) In your imagination you can dine at the White House with this compiled Christmas feast:

A Presidential Christmas Dinner

PRESIDENT AND MRS. WOODROW WILSON	*Roast Turkey*
	Cornbread Stuffing
PRESIDENT AND MRS. JAMES K. POLK	*Tennessee Ham*
PRESIDENT AND MRS. MILLARD FILLMORE	*Whole Stuffed Tomatoes*
PRESIDENT AND MRS. ULYSSES S. GRANT	*Garniture à la Jardinière*
	Hollandaise Sauce
PRESIDENT JAMES BUCHANAN	*Mashed Potatoes*
PRESIDENT AND MRS. FRANKLIN D. ROOSEVELT	*Pecan Pie*
PRESIDENT AND MRS. GEORGE WASHINGTON	*Trifle*
PRESIDENT AND MRS. DWIGHT D. EISENHOWER	*Frosted Mint Delight*
PRESIDENT AND MRS. WARREN G. HARDING	*Almond Cookies*

---

* NOTE TO THE READER: Some of the ingredients in the following recipes have been changed to their modern equivalents, e.g., for *Garniture à la Jardinière* frozen vegetables are used. Of course, those who wish to maintain historical authenticity may want to forgo modern conveniences.

Roast Turkey

(with Cornbread Stuffing)

10- to 12-pound turkey	*Salt, pepper*
Unsalted melted fat	*Paprika*

Wash the turkey inside and out, and pat dry with a cloth. Rub the inside with salt, and fill the body cavity loosely with the stuffing (see below). Secure with skewers.

Place the bird, breast side up, in a roasting pan. Brush the breast, legs, wings with the melted fat.

Preheat oven to 300° F., and roast the turkey, uncovered, in the oven until tender, allowing 25 minutes to the pound. Baste frequently with pan drippings.

When turkey is half cooked, season to taste with salt, pepper, and paprika.

Old Virginia Cornbread Stuffing

Turkey giblets and neck	*3 tablespoons finely chopped*
2 cups boiling water	*onion*
1 bay leaf	*3 tablespoons chopped parsley*
Celery stalks and leaves	*6 tablespoons melted butter*
Salt to taste	*¼ teaspoon pepper*
5 to 6 cups dry cornbread	*1½ cups chopped celery*
crumbs	*Butter*

Cook giblets and neck in 2 cups boiling water with bay leaf, celery stalks and leaves, and salt to taste, until tender. Drain the stock, and reserve. The giblets can be cut up into small pieces and used in the gravy.

Add to the cornbread crumbs, and mix thoroughly, the onion, parsley, melted butter, pepper, and chopped celery. Moisten lightly with the giblet stock. Excess stuffing may be baked separately in a buttered casserole. Dot the top of the mixture with dabs of butter.

PRESIDENT AND MRS. JAMES K. POLK

Tennessee Ham

1 ham	1½ cups brown sugar
1 cup dark molasses	Cracker crumbs
Cloves	Fruit preserves

Completely cover the ham in cold water and soak overnight. Take out and remove any hard surface. Put in suitably sized pot with fresh water, skin side down; add molasses. Cook slowly (225° F.), allowing 25 minutes to the pound. Allow to cool in the liquid. Remove skin carefully. Score ham; stick a clove in each square. Sprinkle with paste made of brown sugar, meal or cracker crumbs, and sufficient liquid to make the paste. Bake slowly in moderate oven (320° F.) for 1 hour, until evenly browned.

Decorate platter with thin ham slices cut from the roast ham, rolled into cornucopias, and filled with fruit preserves.

PRESIDENT AND
MRS. MILLARD FILLMORE

Whole Stuffed Tomatoes

6 firm ripe tomatoes	¼ teaspoon pepper
1½ cups soft bread	2 tablespoons butter or drippings
crumbs	Butter in dabs
1 teaspoon salt	

Select tomatoes of equal size. Cut a piece from the stem end of each, and remove the centers, being careful to keep walls intact. For the stuffing, use the centers of the tomatoes diced, the bread crumbs, seasonings, and the butter or drippings. Mix well. Sprinkle each tomato with salt and pepper, and fill firmly with the stuffing.

Place the tomatoes in a baking dish, with a dab of butter on each. Bake in a moderate oven (350° F. to 375° F.) until tender, about ½ hour. Serve hot.

Garniture à la Jardinière

1 package frozen cauliflower flowerets

1 package frozen asparagus tips

1 package frozen brussels sprouts

2 cups fresh or frozen green peas

1 cup small pearl onions (canned)

1 cup fresh or frozen string beans

2 cups tiny carrots (canned) or frenched carrots

Butter and sugar for glazing

2 boiled turnips, diced

For garnishing: parsley sprigs

Cook all the frozen vegetables according to the directions on each package. Heat all the other vegetables. The carrots should be glazed by sautéing in a bit of butter and sugar. The turnips should be tossed in butter. Arrange the hot vegetables in small mounds on a platter alternating for color. Garnish with parsley. With the vegetables, serve a separate bowl of Hollandaise sauce.

Hollandaise Sauce

2 egg yolks

½ cup butter

¼ teaspoon salt

Dash of cayenne pepper

1½ tablespoons lemon juice

Use a double boiler over water that is hot but not boiling. In top of double boiler, put egg yolks with ⅓ of the butter. Stir mixture constantly. When butter has melted, add another ⅓ of the butter, and as it melts and the mixture thickens, add the remaining ⅓ of the butter. Continue to stir the whole time until the mixture is sufficiently thick; remove from heat and stir in seasonings.

PRESIDENT JAMES BUCHANAN

Mashed Potatoes

3 large Idaho potatoes
salt to taste
¼ teaspoon pepper

2 ounces butter
2 eggs (used separately)
Pastry bag

Peel the potatoes and cut in half. Place in a pan and cover with cold water. Add 1 tablespoon salt, bring to a boil. Let the potatoes simmer until they are soft; drain, return to pan to dry a little. Beat until smooth, adding butter and 1 egg. Season to taste with salt and pepper.

Fill pastry bag with the potato mixture. Use rose tube. Pipe large rosettes on buttered baking dish, sprinkle with beaten egg. Lightly brown under the broiler, watching carefully so that potatoes do not get too brown.

PRESIDENT AND
MRS. FRANKLIN D. ROOSEVELT

Pecan Pie Crust

1½ cups flour
½ teaspoon salt
1 teaspoon baking powder

½ cup shortening
¼ cup ice water

Sift 1½ cups flour with salt and baking powder. Divide shortening into two equal parts. Cut half into the flour mixture until it looks like cornmeal. Cut the remaining half of the shortening coarsely until the size of large green peas. Over the mixture sprinkle 3 tablespoons of ice water. Blend lightly.

If the dough does not hold together, add additional water. Line pie pan with piecrust.

Pecan Pie Filling

1 cup brown sugar
⅓ cup butter
3 or 4 eggs
1 cup light corn syrup
1 cup chopped pecans

1 teaspoon vanilla
¼ teaspoon salt
Pecan halves for garnish
1 pint cream, whipped, for
garnish

Cream ⅓ cup butter with 1 cup brown sugar. Beat in one egg at a time, stir in 1 cup light corn syrup, 1 cup coarsely chopped pecans, 1 teaspoon vanilla, and ¼ teaspoon salt.

Fill the pie shell with the mixture. Preheat the oven to 375° F., and bake the pie for about 35–40 minutes.

When the pie is set and has cooled, decorate the top with pecan halves. Garnish with whipped cream around the entire edge. The whipped cream may be trimmed with tiny leaves baked from leftover small pieces of piecrust dough.

PRESIDENT AND
MRS. GEORGE WASHINGTON

Trifle

Sponge cake, Naples
biscuit, or jelly roll,
cut into slices
½ cup cooking sherry
1 pint heavy cream

1 tablespoon sugar
Rich custard (see below)
Candied fruits and angelica
for decoration

Line the bottom and sides of a deep dish with slices of sponge cake, Naples biscuit, or jelly roll. Wet them with ½ cup cooking sherry. Fill the dish nearly to the top with rich boiled custard (see below).

Sweeten ½ pint of heavy cream with 1 tablespoon sugar; whip to a froth and lay it on the custard. Cover and decorate with the remaining ½ pint whipped cream, preserves of any kind, candied fruits, and angelica.

94

Rich Custard

1 quart milk, scalded
½ cup sugar
Pinch salt
6 eggs, whole

½ cup cold milk
½ teaspoon vanilla or
almond extract

Scald 1 quart milk; add ½ cup sugar, and a pinch of salt. Beat 6 whole eggs and add ½ cup cold milk to them. Stir, gradually add to the hot milk mixture. Cook approximately 5 minutes in top of double boiler until custard coats the spoon. When the custard is cold, add the flavoring.

PRESIDENT AND
MRS. DWIGHT D. EISENHOWER

Frosted Mint Delight

2 1-pound cans crushed pineapple,
reserve 1 cup juice
¾ cup pure mint-flavored
apple jelly
1 envelope unflavored
gelatin

1 pint of whipping cream,
reserve some for garnish
2 teaspoons confectioners'
sugar

Have crushed pineapple and whipping cream chilled. Melt the mint-flavored jelly and mix the crushed pineapple into it. Dissolve the gelatin in 1 cup of the juice from the pineapple. Mix the gelatin mixture and fold it into the pineapple mixture. Now whip the cream, sweeten with the sugar, and fold it into the combined mixture. Put into the freezer until firm, but do not freeze solid.

This recipe serves 10 or 12. Serve in parfait glasses, topped with whipped cream.

PRESIDENT AND
MRS. WARREN G. HARDING

Almond Cookies

1 cup sifted flour
⅓ cup sugar
½ cup grated blanched
    almonds
⅓ cup soft butter

Grated rind of 1 lemon
2 eggs (used separately)
Pinch of salt
Blanched almonds

Sift flour and reserve. Mix sugar, grated almonds, butter, lemon rind, 1 whole egg, and salt together thoroughly with wooden spoon. Gradually work in the sifted flour.

Form the dough into a ball, wrap in wax paper, and chill for at least 1 hour. Now roll out the dough ¼″ thick on a lightly floured board. With cookie cutters cut dough into desired size and shape. Place on greased baking sheet, brush with the other egg, which has been beaten, then decorate each with 3 blanched almonds.

Preheat oven to 350° F. Bake in this moderate oven for about 15 minutes or until light brown.

Christmas Day Grace

TRADITIONAL

A grace for Christmas Day—and every day:

Come, Lord Jesus, be our guest,
Share this food that you have blessed.

THE JOY
OF
GIVING

Somehow Not Only for Christmas

JOHN GREENLEAF WHITTIER

Somehow not only for Christmas
But all the long year through,
The joy that you give to others
Is the joy that comes back to you.

And the more you spend in blessing
The poor and lonely and sad,
The more of your heart's possessing
Returns to make you glad.

This Too I Shall Give

RUTH BELL GRAHAM

This is Christmas—the real meaning of it.
God loving; searching; giving Himself—to us.
Man needing; receiving, giving Himself—to God.
Redemption's glorious exchange of gifts! Without which we cannot live; without which we cannot give to those we love anything of lasting value.
This is the meaning of Christmas—the wonder and the glory of it.

99

God's Gift

BILLY GRAHAM

God is the Giver of the gift. The capability of the donor usually gauges the value of the gift. We don't usually think of a person as a gift, but actually interpersonal relationships are the most valued and cherished gifts of all. But the Bible teaches that God gave a Person as a gift to every one of us, and that Person is Jesus Christ. One day a six-year-old boy in a Southern town answered a knock at the door. It was his father, just returned from Southeast Asia. He didn't ask, "Daddy, what did you bring me?" He threw his arms around his father's neck and said, "Oh, Daddy, this is the best Christmas present I've ever had!"

II Corinthians 9:15

"Thanks be unto God for His unspeakable gift."

What Shall I Give Him?

CHRISTINA G. ROSSETTI

What can I give Him,
*   Poor as I am?*
If I were a shepherd
*   I would bring a lamb,*
If I were a Wise Man
*   I would do my part,—*
Yet what I can I give Him,
*   Give my heart.*

Receive the Gift

RICHARD C. HALVERSON

(Chaplain—U. S. Senate)

Have you received it?
The Christmas Gift . . .
That is, *God's Son?*
Have you *received* Him?
Imagine having your gift turned down . . .
Someone you love greatly—whose gift you *purchased with the profoundest care* . . .
And it is *refused*.
What indescribable disappointment there is in *rejected love*.
God is no less *wounded by our busy indifference*.
If Christmas is not the *receiving of God's Son,* Christmas is nothing!
Were it not for Jesus Christ, there would be no Christmas . . .
Leave Him out and *Christmas is meaningless* . . .
You know it—*it is something to be gotten through*—which, when it is over, leaves you exhausted . . . and often, in debt.
This is not asking you to make your Christmas anything less . . .
This is inviting you to *make it infinitely more*.
Let it be *all God intended*.
Receive the Gift.
Receive *God's Son!*
"For God so loved the world, that He gave His only begotten Son, that whosoever believeth in Him should not perish, but have everlasting life" (John 3:16).
"But as many as received Him, to them gave He power to become the sons of God, even to them that believe on His name" (John 1:12).

The Secret of Happy Giving

CATHERINE MARSHALL

Christmas—the time for giving and receiving gifts—is here again. Nowadays the store decorations go up before Thanksgiving is over. Pondering the commercialism that seems to characterize this holiday season, I began to wonder if the Bible had anything to say about gifts and giving that might be helpful.

When I turned to it, one portion of the Sermon on the Mount seemed especially pertinent. If we stand in the temple, Jesus said,* about to offer a gift to God, and suddenly remember that a friend has a grudge or resentment against us, we are to postpone giving the gift. We are to go and be reconciled to our friend, then come back and offer our gift to God; only then will He receive our offering and bless us. Relationships are primary, He seems to be saying; gifts secondary.

Does this command apply to all gift-giving, I wondered, or only to those gifts labeled expressly for God? With this question in mind I turned to other Scripture passages. I was amazed to see, first, how frequently the giving of gifts is mentioned in the Bible. And second, how in every case the gift springs out of and is symbolic of a relationship, good or bad. Rebekah accepts gifts of jewelry and clothing, symbolic of her acceptance of Isaac as her husband. Jacob tries to give a lavish present of livestock to the brother he has wronged, but Esau refuses. Later on, Jacob singles out one of his sons for the gift of a beautiful coat, demonstrating his favoritism and fostering jealousy among the brothers. Wise Men bring gifts to an Infant—gold which acknowledges their King, frankincense their God, myrrh their Redeemer.

It should not surprise us that the person-to-person dimension is important. The Kingdom of God is the kingdom of right relationships. That's what matters to Him.

When the relationship is right, how precious the gift becomes. I remember the autumn my father spent many weeks making my Christmas gift—a doll bed, dresser and china cupboard. To this day I can shut my eyes and see that miniature furniture, painted white and with glass knobs on the drawers and cupboard doors. But surely the reason I remember it so fondly and in such detail is that the gift spoke of the father-daughter relationship behind it. The handmade furniture said, "I love you; you are important to me—important enough to be worth any amount of my time and my very best effort."

* Matthew 5:23, 24

102

Such gifts are a spontaneous expression of unselfish love. But can we say the same for all the gifts that we give at Christmastime? Isn't it true that sometimes we use the device of a gift to conceal or paper over a flawed relationship? Or—even more common—isn't our attitude sometimes: "I'm giving you this gift because I feel I must (because you expect it, or because you're likely to give me something and I must reciprocate, or because I really don't know how to get out of this bleak and joyless exchange)"?

Perhaps this Christmas all of us should examine our gift list to see if any of our giving falls into that category. If so, why not try the happy experiment of applying Jesus' priority to the situation: first be reconciled to thy brother, then offer thy gift.

We could try it with just one person. As we look down our list, is there anyone for whom we invariably have trouble finding a gift? Is there someone we resent shopping for? Anyone with whom we feel uncomfortable, no matter what we give them? Those can be clues to relationships that need mending.

Once we have selected the person, the next step is to devote time each day to thinking and praying about the relationship. Is the person a neighbor or a co-worker? Perhaps we've never really focused on him as a human being. We have not cared enough even to seek out his needs and preferences. The answer here could be a lunch date, a visit to his home, half an hour of real conversation. Does some old, never-acknowledged resentment lie between us and some member of the family? Healing could take the form of a letter, a face-to-face meeting or simply an interior act of confession.

Whatever the relationship we choose to work on and whatever the steps we take to improve it, we should wait until we are satisfied that it is as close to the one God intended as we can make it. Only then should we proceed with the secondary matter of selecting a gift. The price tag will not matter, as our gift does what all true gifts do—it reflects transparent love.

When we give in that spirit, we are truly making ready for Christmas when Love itself comes down to earth. Then with the Wise Men, we too can kneel at His crib and give thanks for the greatest gift of all.

Christmas Love

Author unknown

Selfishness makes Christmas a burden: love makes it a delight.

If We Had Been There

MARTIN LUTHER

There are some of us . . . who think to ourselves, "If I had only been there! How quick I would have been to help the Baby. I would have washed His linen. How happy I would have been to go with the shepherds to see the Lord lying in the manger!" Yes, we would. We say that because we know how great Christ is, but if we had been there at that time, we would have done no better than the people of Bethlehem . . . Why don't we do it now? We have Christ in our neighbor.

Letter to Hans Christian Andersen

Written by Charles Dickens. December 1847

A thousand thanks, my dear Andersen, for your kind and dearly prized remembrance of me in your Christmas book. I am very proud of it, and feel deeply honored by it, and I cannot tell you how much I esteem so generous a mark of recollection from a man of such genius as you possess.

Your book made my Christmas fireside happier. We were all charmed with it. The little boy, and the old man, and the pewter soldier are my particular favorites. I read that story over and over again, with the most unspeakable delight.

Joy in Giving

JOAN WINMILL BROWN

"It is more blessed to give than to receive." These words kept coming back to me as I gazed into the windows of the elegant stores of London at Christmastime. As a teenager, I desired so much of the dazzling merchandise, but it was going to be a rather meager Christmas; my bank balance had dipped to alarming proportions and I needed so many things for myself. I would have to tell family and friends that it was impossible to exchange gifts this year. "More blessed to give," kept nagging at me as I continued to covet the stores' intriguingly tempting offerings.

I found myself walking through the doors of Liberty's in Regent Street, known for its fine quality—and *high* prices. "I can at least look," I rationalized to myself as I walked past the dignified saleswomen. I felt each one knew just how little money in the vaults of Barclays Bank, at Piccadilly Circus, belonged to me.

Keeping my head held high, I proceeded to look at some of their smaller, more inexpensive gifts. A sachet of potpourri, made of exquisite lace, caught my eye. Instantly it reminded me of my grandmother. How she would love it. I remembered all that her love and understanding had meant to me over the years—I could not let Christmas go by without giving her *something*. Reaching into my wallet I pulled out the necessary money and, forgetting all the things I had needed so badly, began my Christmas shopping.

A joy that had been missing began to surge up inside of me. Perhaps my gifts would not be as expensive as they had been other years, but I was beginning to understand Jesus' words. As I had coveted so many material things for myself, the joy of Christmas had escaped me.

On Christmas Day when I saw the look of happiness on my grandmother's face as she unwrapped her gift, and we looked at each other with love in our eyes that embraced the years of a lifetime of my Christmases . . . I was greatly blessed.

Letter

An excerpt from a letter written by Theodore Roosevelt to James Garfield's grandson. December 26, 1902

Yesterday Archie got among his presents a small rifle from me and a pair of riding boots from his mother. He won't be able to use the rifle until next summer, but he has gone off very happy in the riding boots for a ride on the calico pony Algonquin, the one you rode the other day.

A Glimpse of Christmas Gifts from the Past . . .

GEORGE WASHINGTON

For the Christmas of 1759, President George Washington wrote the following list of presents he wished to give his stepchildren, five-year-old John and three-year-old Patsy.

A bird on Bellows
A Cuckoo
A turnabout Parrot
A Grocers Shop
An Aviary
A Prussian Dragoon
A Man Smoakg
A Tunbridge Tea Sett
3 Neat Tunbridge Toys
A Neat Book fash Tea Chest
A box best Household Stuff
A straw Patch box w. a Glass
A neat dress'd Wax Baby

Excerpt from Diary

An entry in the diary of Princess Victoria, aged 13,
before becoming Queen.
December 24, 1832

After dinner we went upstairs. I then saw Flora, the dog which Sir John was going to give Mamma. Aunt Sophia came also. We then went into the drawing room near the dining room. After Mamma had rung a bell three times we went in. There were two large round tables on which were placed two trees hung with lights and sugar ornaments. All the presents being placed round the tree.

I had one table for myself and the Conroy family had the other together. Lehzen had likewise a little table. Mamma gave me a little lovely pink bag which she had worked with a little sachet likewise done by her; a beautiful little opal brooch and earrings, books, some lovely prints, a pink satin dress and a cloak lined with fur. Aunt Sophia gave me a dress which she worked herself, and Aunt Mary a pair of amethyst earrings. Lehzen a lovely music-book. Victoire a pretty white bag worked by herself, and Sir John a silver brush . . .

Mamma then took me up into my bedroom with all the ladies. There was a new toilet table with a white muslin cover over pink and all my silver things standing on it with a fine new looking-glass. I stayed up till half past 9.

From *Majesty*

ROBERT LACEY

For the Christmas of 1926 the royal family went as usual to Sandringham for the holidays. It was Queen Victoria who had instituted the calendar of peregrinations which took the royal family at Christmas to East Anglia, to Windsor for Easter, and then up to Balmoral in Scotland in August, and King George V followed this routine devotedly. The annual migration was an article of faith "as regular, as unchangeable, as permanent," it seemed to the Duke of Windsor, "as the revolution of a planet in its orbit." On Christmas Eve the estate servants would line up and shuffle forward to receive their gifts—turkeys, hams, beef joints—and a few personal words from their King and Queen. Inside an enormous table would be divided up with ancient ribbons, and the family presents left out on semipermanent display—as Osbert Sitwell discovered when he was reproved for taking his presents upstairs to bed with him. "Members of the royal family were very fond of coming down in any spare moment to gloat over the presents," he noted, "other people's as much as their own."

Christmas at Orchard House

LOUISA MAY ALCOTT

"Christmas won't be Christmas without any presents," grumbled Jo, lying on the rug.

"It's so dreadful to be poor!" sighed Meg, looking down at her old dress.

"I don't think it's fair for some girls to have plenty of pretty things, and other girls nothing at all," added little Amy, with an injured sniff.

"We've got father and mother and each other," said Beth contentedly, from her corner.

The four young faces on which the firelight shone brightened at the cheerful words, but darkened again as Jo said sadly,—

"We haven't got father, and shall not have him for a long time." She didn't say "perhaps never," but each silently added it, thinking of father far away, where the fighting was.

Nobody spoke for a minute; then Meg said in an altered tone, "You know the reason mother proposed not having any presents this Christmas was because it is going to be a hard winter for every one; and she thinks we ought not to spend money for pleasure, when our men are suffering so in the army. We can't do much, but we can make our little sacrifices, and ought to do it gladly. But I'm afraid I don't." And Meg shook her head, as she thought regretfully of all the pretty things she wanted.

"But I don't think the little we should spend would do any good. We've each got a dollar, and the army wouldn't be much helped by our giving that. I agree not to expect anything from mother or you, but I do want to buy *Undine and Sintram* for myself; I've wanted to *so* long," said Jo, who was a bookworm.

"I planned to spend mine in new music," said Beth, with a little sigh, which no one heard but the hearth brush and kettle holder.

"I shall get a nice box of Faber's drawing pencils; I really need them," said Amy decidedly.

"Mother didn't say anything about our money, and she won't wish us to give up everything. Let's each buy what we want, and have a little fun; I'm sure we work hard enough to earn it," cried Jo, examining the heels of her shoes in a gentlemanly manner.

"I know *I* do—teaching those tiresome children nearly all day, when I'm longing to enjoy myself at home," began Meg, in the complaining tone again.

"You don't have half such a hard time as I do," said Jo. "How would you like to be shut up for hours with a nervous, fussy old lady, who keeps you trotting, is never satisfied, and worries you till you're ready to fly out of the window or cry?"

"It's naughty to fret; but I do think washing dishes and keeping things tidy is the worst work in the world. It makes me cross; and my hands get so stiff, I can't practice well at all"; and Beth looked at her rough hands with a sigh that anyone could hear that time.

"I don't believe any of you suffer as I do," cried Amy; "for you don't have to go to school with impertinent girls, who plague you if you don't know your lessons, and laugh at your dresses, and label your father if he isn't rich, and insult you when your nose isn't nice."

"If you mean *libel,* I'd say so, and not talk about *labels,* as if papa was a pickle bottle," advised Jo, laughing.

"I know what I mean, and you needn't be *statirical* about it. It's proper to use good words, and improve your *vocabilary,*" returned Amy, with dignity.

"Don't peck at one another, children. Don't you wish we had the money papa lost when we were little, Jo? Dear me! how happy and good we'd be, if we had no worries!" said Meg, who could remember better times.

"You said, the other day, you thought we were a deal happier than the King children, for they were fighting and fretting all the time, in spite of their money."

"So I did, Beth. Well, I think we are; for, though we do have to work, we make fun for ourselves, and are a pretty jolly set, as Jo would say."

"Jo does use such slang words!" observed Amy, with a reproving look at the long figure stretched on the rug. Jo immediately sat up, put her hands in her pockets, and began to whistle.

"Don't, Jo; it's so boyish!"

"That's why I do it."

"I detest rude, unladylike girls!"

"I hate affected, niminy-piminy chits!"

"'Birds in their little nests agree,'" sang Beth, the peacemaker, with such a funny face that both sharp voices softened to a laugh, and the "pecking" ended for that time.

"Really, girls, you are both to be blamed," said Meg, beginning to lecture in her elder-sisterly fashion. "You are old enough to leave off boyish tricks, and to behave better, Josephine. It didn't matter so much when you were a little girl; but now you are so tall, and turn up your hair, you should remember that you are a young lady."

"I'm not! and if turning up my hair makes me one, I'll wear it in two tails till I'm twenty," cried Jo, pulling off her net, and shaking down a chestnut mane. "I hate to think I've got to grow up, and be Miss March, and wear long gowns, and look as prim as a China-aster! It's bad enough to be a girl, anyway, when I like boys' games and work and manners! I can't get over my disappointment in not being a boy; and it's worse than ever now, for I'm dying to go and fight with papa, and I can only stay at home and knit, like a poky old woman!" And Jo shook the blue army sock till the needles rattled like castanets, and her ball bounded across the room.

"Poor Jo! It's too bad, but it can't be helped; so you must try to be contented with making your name boyish, and playing brother to us girls," said Beth, stroking the rough head at her knee with a hand that all the dishwashing and dusting in the world could not make ungentle in its touch.

"As for you, Amy," continued Meg, "you are altogether too particular and prim. Your airs are funny now; but you'll grow up an affected little goose, if you don't take care. I like your nice manners and refined ways of speaking, when you don't try to be elegant; but your absurd words are as bad as Jo's slang."

"If Jo is a tomboy and Amy a goose, what am I, please?" asked Beth, ready to share the lecture.

"You're a dear, and nothing else," answered Meg warmly; and no one contradicted her, for the "Mouse" was the pet of the family . . .

The clock struck six; and, having swept up the hearth, Beth put a pair of slippers down to warm. Somehow the sight of the old shoes had a good effect upon the girls; for mother was coming, and everyone brightened to welcome her. Meg stopped lecturing, and lighted the lamp. Amy got out of the easy chair without being asked, and Jo forgot how tired she was as she sat up to hold the slippers nearer to the blaze.

"They are quite worn out; Marmee must have a new pair."

"I thought I'd get her some with my dollar," said Beth.

"No, I shall!" cried Amy.

"I'm the oldest," began Meg, but Jo cut in with a decided—"I'm the man of the family now papa is away, and *I* shall provide the slippers, for he told me to take special care of mother while he is gone."

"I'll tell you what we'll do," said Beth; "let's each get her something for Christmas, and not get anything for ourselves."

"That's like you, dear! What will we get?" exclaimed Jo.

Everyone thought soberly for a minute; then Meg announced, as if the idea was suggested by the sight of her own pretty hands, "I shall give her a nice pair of gloves."

"Army shoes, best to be had," cried Jo.

"Some handkerchiefs, all hemmed," said Beth.

"I'll get a little bottle of cologne; she likes it, and it won't cost much, so I'll have some left to buy my pencils," added Amy.

"How will we give the things?" asked Meg.

"Put them on the table, and bring her in and see her open the bundles. Don't you remember how we used to do on our birthdays?" answered Jo.

"I used to be *so* frightened when it was my turn to sit in the big chair with the crown on, and see you all come marching round to give the presents, with a kiss. I liked the things and the kisses, but it was dreadful to have you sit looking at me while I opened the bundles," said Beth, who was toasting her face and the bread for tea, at the same time . . .

Gift Card

JANE MERCHANT

Whatever gift I give you is yours.
Give it away or keep it, as you will.
The special books, the china miniatures,
The little birds carved with beguiling skill—
I shall not peer about your house to see
If they are dusted well and duly shown
To visitors, as treasured things may be.
I made a gift of them and not a loan.

I know that even gifts sincerely loved
Both for themselves and for the giver's sake
Have in life's many changes often proved
A burden; be relieved of the mistake
Of thinking you must keep a gift I give
(Except my love) as long as you shall live.

God, the Giver

DALE EVANS ROGERS

Giving. Always, God is *giving*. Not just on one day do His gifts arrive, but always . . . constantly . . . day by day . . . hour by hour . . . He causes Christmas to happen with the spectacle of little snow-covered trees on mountainsides, in August and July; He trims them with a color and a glory that make our hearts leap up as we behold them. He gives unstintingly and constantly of Christmas beauty to us all, if we have but eyes to see . . .

A Special Gift

HELEN KELLER

The first Christmas after Miss Sullivan came to Tuscumbia was a great event . . . Christmas Eve, after I had hung my stocking. I lay awake a long time, pretending to be asleep and keeping alert to see what Santa Claus would do when he came. At last I fell asleep with a new doll and a white bear in my arms. Next morning it was I who waked the whole family with my first "Merry Christmas!" I found surprises, not in the stocking only, but on the table, on all the chairs, at the door, on the very windowsill; indeed, I could hardly walk without stumbling on a bit of Christmas wrapped up in tissue paper. But when my teacher presented me with a canary, my cup of happiness overflowed.

Little Tim was so tame that he would hop on my finger and eat candied cherries out of my hand. Miss Sullivan taught me to take all the care of my new pet. Every morning after breakfast, I prepared his bath, made his cage clean and sweet, filled his cups with fresh seed and water from the well-house, and hung a spray of chickweed in his swing.

Special Delivery

MRS. CHARLES STEPHAN

Based on a Memphis Commercial Appeal news story by Jack Martin

Delivery boys come in all shapes and sizes—and in a variety of speeds and attitudes too. Some come to the door like beleaguered deliverers of doom while others come on the bound, as though there were more rewards to work than the pay.

David Ward, of Memphis, Tennessee, is the latter kind. Weekdays after school and Saturdays, David pedals his bike for the Speedway Drug Store. And David's a good sort for the job. When he delivers a prescription and says, "I hope you're feeling better" in that polite, concerned way of his, somehow you *do* feel better.

Last year on a Saturday night before Christmas, David, who was thirteen then, received his weekly salary as usual. But he didn't go home. He had a special delivery of his own to make.

First he went down to the lot where the Christmas trees were being sold. When he'd given a number of the trees his careful inspection, he bought one and loaded it on his bicycle. Then he wheeled it over to 605 Life Street, the home of a steady customer, Mrs. Brady Neals. She was seventy-one. And she had been blind for thirty-seven years.

"It's me, Mrs. Neals, David from Speedway," he said when she came to the door. And then David walked in and set up the tree and talked cheerily as he trimmed it with the lights and decorations he had brought along.

Mrs. Neals could hardly speak. Even as David was leaving she could only mumble her thanks. But the old lady was thrilled. She kept reaching out to touch the tree's branches and to breathe its forest-fresh fragrance. "I'm seventy-one years old," she kept saying over and over, "Im seventy-one years old and I've never had a tree."

Delivery boys come in all shapes and sizes and some of them bring more to their jobs than work.

A Hint for Next Christmas

A. A. MILNE

. . . I am reminded of the ingenuity of a friend of mine, William by name, who arrived at a large country house for Christmas without any present in his bag. He had expected neither to give nor to receive anything, but to his horror he discovered on the twenty-fourth that everybody was preparing a Christmas present for him, and that it was taken for granted that he would require a little privacy and brown paper on Christmas Eve for the purpose of addressing his own offerings to others. He had wild thoughts of telegraphing to London for something to be sent down, and spoke to other members of the house party in order to discover what sort of presents would be suitable.

"What are you giving our host?" he asked . . .

"Mary and I are giving him a book," said John, referring to his wife.

William then approached the youngest son of the house, and discovered that he and his next brother Dick were sharing in this, that, and the other. When he had heard this, William retired to his room and thought profoundly.'

He was the first down to breakfast on Christmas morning. All the places at the table were piled high with presents. He looked at John's plate. The top parcel said, "To John and Mary from Charles." William took out his fountain pen and added a couple of words to the inscription. It then read, "To John and Mary from Charles and William," and in William's opinion looked just as effective as before. He moved on to the next place. "To Angela from Father," said the top parcel. "And William," wrote William. At his hostess' place he hesitated for a moment. The first present there was for "Darling Mother, from her loving children." It did not seem that an "and William" was quite suitable. But his hostess was not to be deprived of William's kindly thought; twenty seconds later the handkerchiefs "from John and Mary and William" expressed all the nice things which he was feeling for her. He passed on to the next place . . .

It is of course impossible to thank every donor of a joint gift; one simply thanks the first person whose eye one happens to catch. Sometimes William's eye was caught, sometimes not. But he was spared all embarrassment; and I can recommend his solution of the problem with a perfect confidence to those who may be in a similar predicament . . .

The Gift of the Magi

O. HENRY

One dollar and eighty-seven cents. That was all. And sixty cents of it was in pennies. Pennies saved one and two at a time by bulldozing the grocer and the vegetable man and the butcher until one's cheeks burned with the silent imputation of parsimony that such close dealing implied. Three times Della counted it. One dollar and eighty-seven cents. And the next day would be Christmas.

There was clearly nothing to do but flop down on the shabby little couch and howl. So Della did it. Which instigates the moral reflection that life is made up of sobs, sniffles, and smiles, with sniffles predominating.

While the mistress of the home is gradually subsiding from the first stage to the second, take a look at the home. A furnished flat at $8 per week. It did not exactly beggar description, but it certainly had that word on the lookout for the mendicancy squad.

In the vestibule below was a letter-box into which no letter would go, and an electric button from which no mortal finger could coax a ring. Also appertaining thereunto was a card bearing the name "Mr. James Dillingham Young."

The "Dillingham" had been flung to the breeze during a former period of prosperity when its possessor was being paid $30 per week. Now, when the income was shrunk to $20, the letters of "Dillingham" looked blurred, as though they were thinking seriously of contracting to a modest and unassuming D. But whenever Mr. James Dillingham Young came home and reached his flat above he was called "Jim" and greatly hugged by Mrs. James Dillingham Young, already introduced to you as Della. Which is all very good.

Della finished her cry and attended to her cheeks with the powder rag. She stood by the window and looked out dully at a gray cat walking a gray fence in a gray backyard. Tomorrow would be Christmas Day, and she had only $1.87 with which to buy Jim a present. She had been saving every penny she could for months, with this result. Twenty dollars a week doesn't go far. Expenses had been greater than she had calculated. They always are. Only $1.87 to buy a present for Jim. Her Jim. Many a happy hour she had spent planning for something nice for him. Something fine and rare and sterling—something just a little bit near to being worthy of the honor of being owned by Jim.

There was a pier-glass between the windows of the room. Perhaps you have seen a pier-glass in an $8 flat. A very thin and very agile person may, by observing his reflection in a rapid sequence of longitudinal strips, obtain a fairly accurate conception of his looks. Della, being slender, had mastered the art.

Suddenly she whirled from the window and stood before the glass. Her eyes were shining brilliantly, but her face had lost its color within twenty seconds. Rapidly she pulled down her hair and let it fall to its full length.

Now, there were two possessions of the James Dillingham Youngs in which they both took a mighty pride. One was Jim's gold watch that had been his father's and his grandfather's. The other was Della's hair. Had the Queen of Sheba lived in the flat across the airshaft, Della would have let her hair hang out the window some day to dry just to depreciate Her Majesty's jewels and gifts. Had King Solomon been the janitor, with all his treasures piled up in the basement, Jim would have pulled out his watch every time he passed, just to see him pluck at his beard from envy.

So now Della's beautiful hair fell about her, rippling and shining like a cascade of brown waters. It reached below her knee and made itself almost a garment for her. And then she did it up again nervously and quickly. Once she faltered for a minute and stood still while a tear or two splashed on the worn red carpet.

On went her old brown jacket; on went her old brown hat. With a whirl of skirts and with the brilliant sparkle still in her eyes, she fluttered out the door and down the stairs to the street.

Where she stopped the sign read: "Mme. Sofronie. Hair Goods of All Kinds." One flight up Della ran, and collected herself, panting. Madame, large, too white, chilly, hardly looked the "Sofronie."

"Will you buy my hair?" asked Della.

"I buy hair," said Madame. "Take yer hat off and let's have a sight at the looks of it."

Down rippled the brown cascade.

"Twenty dollars," said Madame, lifting the mass with a practiced hand.

"Give it to me quick," said Della.

Oh, and the next two hours tripped by on rosy wings. Forget the hashed metaphor. She was ransacking the stores for Jim's present.

She found it at last. It surely had been made for Jim and no one else. There was no other like it in any of the stores, and she had turned all of them inside out. It was a platinum fob chain simple and chaste in design, properly proclaiming its value by substance alone and not by meretricious ornamentation—as all good things should do. It was even worthy of The Watch. As soon as she saw it she knew that it must be Jim's. It was like him. Quietness and value—the description applied to both. Twenty-one dollars they took from her for it, and she hurried home with the 87 cents. With that chain on his watch Jim might be properly anxious about the time in any company. Grand as the watch was, he sometimes looked at it on the sly on account of the old leather strap that he used in place of a chain.

When Della reached home her intoxication gave way a little to prudence and reason. She got out her curling irons and lighted the gas and went to work repairing the ravages made by generosity added to love. Which is always a tremendous task, dear friends—a mammoth task.

Within forty minutes her head was covered with tiny, close-lying curls that made her look wonderfully like a truant schoolboy. She looked at her reflection in the mirror long, carefully, and critically.

"If Jim doesn't kill me," she said to herself, "before he takes a second look at me, he'll say I look like a Coney Island chorus girl. But what could I do—oh! what could I do with a dollar and eighty-seven cents?"

At 7 o'clock the coffee was made and the frying-pan was on the back of the stove hot and ready to cook the chops.

Jim was never late. Della doubled the fob chain in her hand and sat on the corner of the table near the door that he always entered. Then she heard his step on the stair away down on the first flight, and she turned white for just a moment. She had a habit of saying little silent prayers about the simplest everyday things, and now she whispered: "Please, God, make him think I am still pretty."

The door opened and Jim stepped in and closed it. He looked thin and very serious. Poor fellow, he was only twenty-two—and to be burdened with a family! He needed a new overcoat and he was without gloves.

Jim stopped inside the door, as immovable as a setter at the scent of quail. His eyes were fixed upon Della, and there was an expression in them that she could not read, and it terrified her. It was not anger, nor surprise, nor disapproval, nor horror, nor any of the sentiments that she had been prepared for. He simply stared at her fixedly with that peculiar expression on his face.

Della wriggled off the table and went for him.

"Jim, darling," she cried, "don't look at me that way. I had my hair cut off and sold it because I couldn't have lived through Christmas without giving you a present. It'll grow out again—you won't mind, will you? I just had to do it. My hair grows awfully fast. Say 'Merry Christmas!' Jim, and let's be happy. You don't know what a nice—what a beautiful, nice gift I've got for you."

"You've cut off your hair?" asked Jim, laboriously, as if he had not arrived at that patent fact even after the hardest mental labor.

"Cut it off and sold it," said Della. "Don't you like me just as well, anyhow? I'm me without my hair, ain't I?"

Jim looked about the room curiously.

"You say your hair is gone?" he said, with an air almost of idiocy.

"You needn't look for it," said Della. "It's sold, I tell you—sold and gone, too. It's Christmas Eve, boy. Be good to me, for it went for you. Maybe the hairs of my head were numbered," she went on with a sudden serious sweetness, "but nobody could ever count my love for you. Shall I put the chops on, Jim?"

Out of his trance Jim seemed quickly to wake. He enfolded his Della. For ten seconds let us regard with discreet scrutiny some inconsequential object in the other direction. Eight dollars a week or a million a year—what is the difference? A mathematician or a wit would give you the wrong answer. The magi brought valuable gifts, but that was not among them. This dark assertion will be illuminated later on.

Jim drew a package from his overcoat pocket and threw it upon the table.

"Don't make any mistake, Dell," he said, "about me. I don't think there's anything in the way of a haircut or a shave or a shampoo that could make me like my girl any less. But if you'll unwrap that package you may see why you had me going a while at first."

White fingers and nimble tore at the string and paper. And then an ecstatic scream of joy; and then, alas! a quick feminine change to hysterical tears and wails, necessitating the immediate employment of all the comforting powers of the lord of the flat.

For there lay The Combs—the set of combs, side and back, that Della had worshiped for long in a Broadway window. Beautiful combs, pure tortoiseshell, with jeweled rims—just the shade to wear in the beautiful vanished hair. They were expensive combs, she knew, and her heart had simply craved and yearned over them without the least hope of possession. And now, they were hers, but the tresses that should have adorned the coveted adornments were gone.

But she hugged them to her bosom, and at length she was able to look up with dim eyes and a smile and say: "My hair grows so fast, Jim!"

And then Della leaped up like a little singed cat and cried, "Oh, oh!"

Jim had not yet seen his beautiful present. She held it out to him eagerly upon her open palm. The dull precious metal seemed to flash with a reflection of her bright and ardent spirit.

"Isn't it a dandy, Jim? I hunted all over town to find it. You'll have to look at the time a hundred times a day now. Give me your watch. I want to see how it looks on it."

119

Instead of obeying, Jim tumbled down on the couch and put his hands under the back of his head and smiled.

"Dell," said he, "let's put our Christmas presents away and keep 'em a while. They're too nice to use just at present. I sold the watch to get the money to buy your combs. And now suppose you put the chops on."

The magi, as you know, were wise men—wonderfully wise men—who brought gifts to the Babe in the manger. They invented the art of giving Christmas presents. Being wise, their gifts were no doubt wise ones, possibly bearing the privilege of exchange in case of duplication. And here I have lamely related to you the uneventful chronicle of two foolish children in a flat who most unwisely sacrificed for each other the greatest treasures of their house. But in a last word to the wise of these days let it be said that of all who give gifts these two were the wisest. Of all who give and receive gifts, such as they are wisest. Everywhere they are wisest. They are the magi.

Johnny and June Cash are known for their generosity and concern for others. Children, prisoners, those in need are not forgotten by this dedicated and talented couple. They know that of all the gifts, love is the best. On a TV Christmas special, Johnny recited this favorite poem of his:

The Christmas Guest

Traditional Poem—Author unknown
Additional words by Grandpa Jones and Bill Walker

It happened one day near December's end,
Two neighbors called on an old-time friend,
And they found his shop so meager and mean,
Made gay with a thousand boughs of green,
And Conrad was sitting with face a-shine—
When he suddenly stopped as he stitched a twine
And said, "Old friends, at dawn today
When the cock was crowing the night away—
The Lord appeared in a dream to me—

And said, 'I am coming your guest to be,'
So I've been busy with feet astir
Strewing my shop with branches of fir.
The table is spread and the kettle is shined
And over the rafters the holly is twined—
And now I will wait for my Lord to appear
And listen closely so I will hear
His step as he nears my humble place—
And I open the door and look on his face."
So his friends went home and left Conrad alone,
For this was the happiest day he had known.
For long since his family had passed away (pause)
And Conrad had spent many a sad Christmas Day.
But he knew with the Lord as his Christmas guest,
This Christmas would be the dearest and best.
So he listened with only joy in his heart,
And with every sound he would rise with a start
And look for the Lord to be at the door
Like the vision he had a few hours before.
So he ran to the window after hearing a sound,
But all he could see on the snow-covered ground
Was a shabby beggar whose shoes were torn—
And all of his clothes were ragged and worn;
But Conrad was touched and went to the door,
And he said, "Your feet must be frozen and sore—
I have some shoes in my shop for you,
And a coat that will keep you warmer, too."
So with grateful heart the man went away—
But Conrad noticed the time of day;
He wondered what made the dear Lord so late
And how much longer he'd have to wait—
When he heard a knock and ran to the door,
But it was only a stranger once more,
A bent old lady with a shawl of black,
With a bundle of kindling piled on her back.
She asked for only a place to rest—
But that was reserved for Conrad's great guest,
But her voice seemed to plead, "Don't send me away,
Let me rest for a while on Christmas Day."
So Conrad brewed her a steaming cup
And told her to sit at the table and sup.
But after she left, he was filled with dismay,
For he saw that the hours were slipping away,
And the Lord had not come as he said he would

121

And Conrad felt sure he had misunderstood.
When out of the stillness he heard a cry,
"Please help me and tell me where am I."
So again he opened his friendly door.
And stood disappointed as twice before.
It was only a child who had wandered away
And was lost from her family on Christmas Day.
Again Conrad's heart was heavy and sad
But he knew he could make this little girl glad.
So he called her in and wiped her tears
And quieted all her childish fears,
Then he led her back to her home once more,
But as he entered his own darkened door,
He knew that the Lord was not coming today
For the hours of Christmas had passed away.
So he went to his room and knelt down to pray,
And he said, "Lord, why did you delay,
What kept you from coming to call on me,
For I wanted so much your face to see."
When soft in the silence, a voice he heard,
"Lift up your head for I kept my word.
Three times my shadow crossed your floor,
Three times I came to your lowly door;
For I was the beggar with bruised cold feet;
I was the woman you gave something to eat,
And I was the child on the homeless street;
Three times I knocked, three times I came in,
And each time I found the warmth of a friend.
Of all the gifts, love is the best;
I was honored to be your Christmas Guest."

The Real Spirit of Christmas

CALVIN COOLIDGE

Christmas is not a time nor a season, but a state of mind. To cherish peace and goodwill, to be plenteous in mercy, is to have the real spirit of Christmas.

The Christmas Heart

GEORGE MATTHEW ADAMS

The Christmas heart is a beautiful heart for it is full of love and thoughtfulness for others.

And the Christmastime is a tribute to the most beautiful heart that ever beat.

It is also the time in which we are brought closest to our own inadequate abilities and helplessness of spirit. For we are so bathed with unselfishness that we feel our failures and lacks as never before in the entire year.

Perhaps it is well this way, so that we may resolve anew to live better and stronger lives for those who mean so much to us.

So let us cherish this Christmas heart and keep it a Christmas heart all through the year to come.

Let us put on all the lights in this heart so that it will be aglow to the world and let us push up the shades of the windows in this heart so that everyone who passes may be cheered and inspired.

Let us remember that the Christmas heart is a giving heart, a wide-open heart that thinks of others first.

The birth of the baby Jesus stands as the most significant event in all history, because it has meant the pouring into a sick world of the healing medicine of love which has transformed all manner of hearts for almost two thousand years and given beauty to human service it would never have had otherwise.

Underneath all the bulging bundles is this beating Christmas heart. Enwrapped about the tiniest gift is this same loveliness of thought and heart expression.

What a happy New Year for all if we would carry this same Christmas heart into every day during the coming year and make it a permanent thing in our lives. Let's do it!

THE JOY
OF
MUSIC

All My Heart This Night Rejoices

PAUL GERHARDT

All my heart this night rejoices,
As I hear,
Far and near,
Sweetest angel voices:
"Christ is born" their choirs are singing,
Till the air,
Everywhere,
Now with joy is ringing.

Johann Sebastian Bach's Christmas Oratorio

"The object of all music should be to the glory of God," observed Bach. Those who have listened and been moved by this composer's magnificent music would agree that all of Bach's compositions glorify the Creator.

The jubilant *Christmas Oratorio* with its lyrical commentary unfolds the Gospel narrative. It literally bursts forth with irrepressible joy.

The work was first performed between Christmas Day, 1734, and

Epiphany, 1735. The opening chorus is a stupendous creation and is said to have been completed by Bach in thirty-six hours.

All the magnificence, the hope and joy of Christmas fill our very beings as we listen to this devout composer's inspired music celebrating our Lord's birth.

Christians be joyful, and praise your salvation,
Christians be joyful, and praise your salvation,
Sing for today your Redeemer is born;
Cease to be fearful, forget lamentation,
Cease to be fearful, forget lamentation,
Haste with thanksgiving to greet this glad morn!

Christmas at the Bachs'

A. E. BRACHVOGEL

From Friedemann Bach
Translated by Anne Fremantle

It was the morning of Christmas Eve. The days are then astonishingly short. One can hardly get down to a job before it's dark again, and yet father and son need the daylight so badly for their work! In the living room Friedemann and Sebastian are sitting at a table, which has been pulled up in front of the window. Each has a shining copperplate in front of him, set upon an old windowseat cushion for a pad, upon which the copperplate rotates while the gleaming metal stylus etches deep, restlessly moving back and forth, and digging out measures, intervals and cadenzas on the already marked staves of the original MSS. Sebastian Bach, too poor to have the work done by an engraver, too little a follower of the modern trend in music fashion to find a publisher—this same Sebastian Bach painfully engraves the whole *Art of the Fugue* with his son, so that his life's masterpiece shall not be lost.

The old man's mouth is twisted bitterly. Yes, yes, he is no Hasse, no Rameau, no Couperin or Chiabran. He does not write operas or dear little canzonettas! Who would buy church music today, or even listen to it? Gradually, the century prepares to erase the Lord God from His universe, so who would have a taste for His hymns?

The old man is wearing green glasses. Can't you see how rheumy his eyes are? The blinding brightness of the copper burns them, and he may go blind before he has succeeded in casting the ephemeral tones he creates into permanence for posterity. Quiet Anna Magdalena decorates the Christmas tree in the schoolroom, Friedrich and Christian are still at school, and David is sitting on the floor, playing with scraps of paper which he throws high up into the air. He is making "pigeons fly."

"I wonder how Old Nicolas and Fredericka are faring in Naumburg?" says the father, who had to interrupt his work to sharpen his instrument and wipe his glasses. "They haven't written for quite some time. I thought perhaps they would have come to Leipzig for Christmas."

"How can they be anything but well?" replies Friedemann without looking up. "They have their own home, a good job—oh, indeed, everything must go well with them."

His father looks at Friedemann, and then the conversation was already at an end. Every time their talk got onto any subject other than their work, the evil spirits of envy and anguish, which raged within the son, closed his father's lips. Even the most innocent banter was thus poisoned. Finally, the father put down his stylus with an authoritative air.

"Friedemann," he said, "it's just no good. Your misfortunes make you wicked and envious. You cling far too stubbornly to your melancholy, and you will isolate yourself more and more from your fellow men. If you were truly religious, you would know that in the end God works everything out well, and that faith would give you the strength to lift yourself above your sorrow, and hope, in its turn, would give you the strength to work cheerfully."

"But, dear Father, am I not doing all I possibly can? What else is there I can do?"

"Just making such an effort, Friedemann, will not help you. You are only torturing yourself by trying to force yourself. That's why you don't succeed. Without joy, without hope, any work of art is stillborn. It becomes more and more clear to me that you don't have the basic essentials of religious faith. You are lacking in the spirit of service, which finds creative strength in its very humility. Today our Lord is born, the Savior of our poor human race. Oh, if only God would give me the joy of knowing that a Savior was born in you, too, who would set you free from yourself, and would give you new heart, new courage! For then, my dear son, everything would work out, believe me. All of us, and you yourself, would together find our happiness in you."

In spite of himself he had begun to cry, and he silently embraced his son. It was a last cry wrung from his paternal heart. Friedemann could hardly bear it. Gently he pushed his father aside. "Wait just one moment, dear Father, I'll be right back." He rushed out of the room in order to hide his emotion. Sebastian was left to his sad thoughts, while David played quietly at his feet. The old man put his hands together as though in a despairing prayer, and turned his burning eyes toward the window, and out, up to the gray sky full of swirling snowflakes.

Shortly after Friedemann entered the room quietly. He was very pale, and in his hand he was holding a sheet with music on it.

"Here, Father, I have made one last attempt. I was going to give it to you tonight, but since you and I are so sad I thought perhaps that this is the best moment."

Sebastian pressed his hand. He was trembling as he took the composition and spread it out suspiciously. Dear God, how the fear of false hope showed in his face! His son watched him closely, as though his father were about to pass a sentence of death upon him. Sebastian's face was flushed a deep red. He looked now at Friedemann, now at the paper, as though he were in a dream.

"Oh, Father, it is bad, isn't it?"

"Bad? Are you crazy? No, my dearest, it's good, so good and so beautiful, that if you will forgive me for saying so, I can't really quite believe that it is yours." As he spoke, a blissful joy, all his old pride in his Friedemann, came back into Sebastian's heart with heady jubilation. Sobbing and laughing at the same time, like a child, he embraced his son and rushed out to the boy's mother, waving the music high in the air in front of him.

Friedemann felt reborn. The sun of his old self-confidence began to warm his sick heart, and rosy hope softly opened the doors of its temple, through which his trembling soul advanced furtively. He followed his father. There, in the schoolroom, the old man was already at the piano, and he played the introduction, while mother Magdalena in her dear voice was singing the hymn which rose up to our Lord like a prayer.

On earth grows no small blade,
But heaven has dew besprint
Each small flower in the shade.
Still the sun's gold does glint,
And when your self finds you
Alone in forest night,
Your dew and sunshine, too,
Will pour upon you bright.
Then shoots shall blossom green
From out your deepest heart,
For no live thing is seen
But flowering is its part.

His mother was beside herself with joy. She laughed and cried, and the father played and hummed the hymn again and again, and could not get his fill of it. Finally he jumped up. "Tell me, dear son, wherever in all the world did you find the beautiful poem? And how glorious the music is!"

"I wrote the poem, too, Father."

"Oh, you see, Mother, how the old strength is still in him! This came straight from his very soul, it is part of his very self, and that is why it is so magnificent and mighty! Take courage, dearest Friedemann, and don't be moody any more, because the old Lord is still alive, and today he has sent you the genuine, most beautiful Christ child, Who is your own Savior, and without Whom we cannot exist in this our life."

And that is how it was. Friedemann smiled again, and the old blessed spirit of love, rosy self-confidence with its shy smile, dwelt with him again. Today is the Christ feast, and it was caroled throughout the house as of old. Familiar voices called "Christ's feast," and there, standing on the threshold, was dear Fredericka holding two blond children and there was cheerful Old Nicolas.

"Come in, come in," said Sebastian happily, "that my house may be filled." And greetings and kisses and joy and tears were all mixed up, because once again it was like in the old days. The days of sorrow were forgotten, or melted away into the hours of joy, into the hope of happy days. And once again the door opened, and in came Mietzler, with a deputation from the society of the musical sciences, and presented Sebastian with an honorary membership in the name of all the musicians.

"You know, Mother, when heaven sends you joy, it does so thoroughly, and I must thank God and praise this day, when I can be truly happy, from the bottom of my heart, after the long days of sorrow. And Friedemann, you, too, must help me. Come, put your thinking cap on! We will write a Christmas song, and the society shall have it right away, so that they may learn what kind of new member they are getting. Come, dear boy."

Evening came. The Christmas tree shone in fairy splendor, the lovely legend of the Love that descended from heaven for the salvation and freedom and brotherhood of the divided world wove its golden web once more around the mourning hearts of a sorrowful mankind. There, at the instrument, in the magical twinkling light of the Christmas tree, sat the old bard, in a frenzy of enthusiasm, with his wife, his child, and his child's child. And all were singing the Christmas song:

Be not afraid; look ye,
for I bring unto you joyful tidings
which shall be to all people.
For unto you there is born this day
in the city of David a Savior which is
    Christ the Lord.

The old carol singer has long been sleeping in the kingdom of peace, but his immortal song still clarions forth in our hearts, and they become young and new when the organ plays on Christmas night:

    For I bring unto you joyful tidings.

Rejoice and Sing

JOHANN SEBASTIAN BACH

Rejoice, and sing. Rejoice and sing.
Your gracious King. As Man is born,
And lays aside His glory; He is ador'd,
As Christ and Lord, And every tongue
repeats the wondrous story.

Carols in Gloucestershire

From "Cider with Rosie"

LAURIE LEE

. . . Mile after mile we went, fighting against the wind, falling into snowdrifts, and navigating by the lights of the houses. And yet we never saw our audience. We called at house after house; we sang in courtyards and porches, outside windows, or in the damp gloom of hallways; we heard voices from hidden rooms; we smelled rich clothes and strange hot food; we saw maids bearing in dishes or carrying away coffee cups; we received nuts, cakes, figs, preserved ginger, dates, cough drops and money; but never once saw our patrons. We sang as it were at the castle walls, and apart from the squire, who had shown himself to prove that he was still alive, we never expected it otherwise.

As the night drew on there was trouble with Boney. "Noel," for instance, had a rousing harmony which Boney persisted in singing, and singing flat. The others forbade him to sing it at all, and Boney said he would fight us. Picking himself up, he agreed we were right, then he disappeared altogether. He just turned away and walked into the snow and wouldn't answer when we called him back. Much later, as we reached a far point up the valley, somebody said "Hark!" and we stopped to listen. Far away across the fields from the distant village came the sound of a frail voice singing, singing "Noel," and singing it flat —it was Boney, branching out on his own.

We approached our last house high up on the hill, the place of Joseph the farmer. For him we had chosen a special carol, which was about the other Joseph, so that we always felt that singing it added a spicy cheek to the night. The last stretch of country to reach his farm was perhaps the most difficult of all. In these rough bare lanes, open to all winds, sheep were buried and wagons lost. Huddled together, we tramped in one another's footsteps, powdered snow blew into our screwed-up eyes, the candles burned low, some blew out altogether, and we talked loudly above the gale.

Crossing, at last, the frozen millstream—whose wheel in summer still turned a barren mechanism—we climbed up to Joseph's farm. Sheltered by trees, warm on its bed of snow, it seemed always to be like this. As always it was late; as always this was our final call. The snow had a fine crust upon it, and the old trees sparkled like tinsel.

We grouped ourselves round the farmhouse porch. The sky cleared, and broad streams of stars ran down over the valley and away to Wales. On Slad's white slopes, seen through the black sticks of its woods, some red lamps still burned in the windows.

Everything was quiet; everywhere there was the faint crackling silence of the winter night. We started singing, and we were all moved by the words and the sudden trueness of our voices. Pure, very clear, and breathless we sang:

> *As Joseph was a-walking*
> *He heard an angel sing:*
> *"This night shall be the birth time*
> *Of Christ the Heavenly King.*
>
> *"He neither shall be born*
> *In house nor in hall,*
> *Nor in a place of paradise*
> *But in an ox's stall . . ."*

And two thousand Christmases became real to us then; the houses, the halls, the places of paradise had all been visited; the stars were bright to guide the Kings through the snow; and across the farmyard we could hear the beasts in their stalls. We were given roast apples and hot mince pies, in our nostrils were spices like myrrh, and in our wooden box, as we headed back for the village, there were golden gifts for all.

I Heard the Bells on Christmas Day

HENRY WADSWORTH LONGFELLOW

As Henry Wadsworth Longfellow was listening to the ringing of the Christmas bells in Cambridge, Massachusetts, in 1863, deep feelings and memories began stirring within him. It was only six months after the Battle of Gettysburg: the nation was mourning the loss of so many loved ones during the Civil War. Longfellow's young son, a lieutenant in the Army of the Potomac, had been seriously wounded.

His thoughts turned to peace. The words from Luke, ". . . on earth peace, goodwill toward men," inspired him to write this well-loved poem.

> *I heard the bells on Christmas Day*
> *Their old, familiar carols play,*
> *And wild and sweet*
> *The words repeat*
> *Of peace on earth, good-will to men!*
>
> *And thought how, as the day had come,*
> *The belfries of all Christendom*
> *Had rolled along*
> *Th' unbroken song*
> *Of peace on earth, good-will to men!*
>
> *And in despair I bowed my head;*
> *"There is no peace on earth," I said,*
> *"For hate is strong,*
> *And mocks the song*
> *Of peace on earth, good-will to men!"*
>
> *Then pealed the bells more loud and deep,*
> *"God is not dead, nor doth He sleep!*
> *The Wrong shall fail,*
> *The Right prevail,*
> *With peace on earth, good-will to men!"*

Silent Night

JOSEPH MOHR AND FRANZ GRUBER

The song "Silent Night" echoed out of the small village of Oberndorf in the Tyrolean Alps of Austria. The twenty-five-year-old rector of the village church, Joseph Mohr, was alone on Christmas Eve, 1818, when he heard a loud pounding on the door. He opened the door and a woman pushed past him gasping, "Come, a child is born, and the young father and mother want you to bless their home." Then the woman collapsed from exhaustion.

The rector started out on a tedious journey up the mountainside, to a small cabin, miles in distance. After many hours of climbing he reached his destination and saw within the cabin a repetition of the Nativity scene. The young woman lay on a bed of boughs, and her newborn son lay in a roughhewn cradle made by the Alpine-mountaineer father. The rector blessed the home and left the cabin to make a return journey to the village. His heart filled with song, because of the uplifting impressive scene; and his ears filled with the rapturous tune which enveloped him. Keeping his feet in rhythm he made his way down the mountainside. That Christmas night the rector stayed up writing the manuscript for his inspired song.

The next morning Joseph Mohr visited the village organist and choirmaster, Franz Gruber. He asked the choirmaster to pick out the melody for the song on an old guitar because the organ was broken. A few hours later Franz Gruber ran to the rectory with the tune and the words he had sounded out. On December 25, 1818, the villagers of Oberndorf gathered in the rectory to hear for the first time the song "Silent Night," sung by Joseph Mohr and Franz Gruber. It was a song of peace.

Silent night! holy night!
Guiding Star, lend thy light!
See the eastern Wise Men bring
Gifts and homage to our King!
Christ the Savior is born,
Christ the Savior is born.

Silent night! holy night!
Wondrous Star, lend thy light!
With the angels let us sing
Alleluia to our King!
Christ the Savior is born,
Christ the Savior is born.

Away in a Manger

Attributed to Martin Luther

Although there is no proof that Martin Luther wrote this carol, it is often referred to as "Luther's Cradle Hymn." This carol lullaby is sung throughout the world and encourages children to love "the little Lord Jesus."

The importance of teaching children about the Savior was vividly and poignantly illustrated when Kathryn Koob was taken hostage in Iran in 1979. Through her Christian education at an early age and her love for Jesus Christ, she found the strength and comfort she needed to live through her ordeal. At Christmas 1980 her captors inadvertently allowed her to speak of that faith to the nation and to her family on television. She sent her greetings and then sang the third verse of this carol, one she had learned and loved as a child.

On Kathryn Koob's return to the United States she was asked many times whether she chose this verse because she was depressed, thinking she might die and go to heaven. "I can't imagine heaven being depressing under any circumstances. I just wanted to share a prayer with the world, and with my family—with my nieces and nephews."

One of the simplest of all carols, it is also one of the most loved because we first learned it as children.

> *Away in a manger, no crib for a bed,*
> *The little Lord Jesus laid down His sweet head;*
> *The stars in the sky looked down where He lay,*
> *The little Lord Jesus, asleep on the hay.*
>
> *The cattle are lowing, the Baby awakes,*
> *But little Lord Jesus, no crying He makes;*
> *I love Thee, Lord Jesus! look down from the sky,*
> *And stay by my cradle till morning is nigh.*
>
> *Be near me, Lord Jesus, I ask Thee to stay*
> *Close by me forever, and love me, I pray;*
> *Bless all the dear children in Thy tender care,*
> *And fit us for heaven to live with Thee there.*

O Little Town of Bethlehem

PHILLIPS BROOKS

On Christmas Eve in Bethlehem in 1865, a young minister was deeply moved by a simple church service commemorating Christ's birth. As he stood in the ancient building, which dated back to the fourth century, little did Phillips Brooks realize that just a few years later the memory of that scene would be used by him to write one of the most beautiful Christmas carols.

In 1868, while minister of Holy Trinity, Philadelphia, he was approached by one of the children who attended the church school to write them a special Christmas song. Sitting down, he remembered the peaceful scene of Bethlehem, with the shepherds' field close by, and in one evening wrote the simple but meaningful verses that tell of God's incredible gift to mankind. Brooks asked his church organist to compose the music—together they gave us a carol that is a favorite in many countries.

> O little town of Bethlehem,
> How still we see thee lie!
> Above thy deep and dreamless sleep
> The silent stars go by;
> Yet in thy dark streets shineth
> The everlasting Light;
> The hopes and fears of all the years
> Are met in thee tonight.
>
> For Christ is born of Mary,
> And gathered all above,
> While mortals sleep, the angels keep
> Their watch of wondering love.
> O morning stars, together
> Proclaim the holy birth!
> And praises sing to God the King,
> And peace to men on earth.
>
> How silently, how silently,
> The wondrous gift is giv'n!
> So God imparts to human hearts
> The blessings of His heav'n.

No ear may hear His coming,
But in this world of sin,
Where meek souls will receive Him, still
The dear Christ enters in.

O holy Child of Bethlehem!
Descend to us, we pray;
Cast out our sin and enter in,
Be born in us today.
We hear the Christmas angels
The great glad tidings tell;
O come to us, abide with us,
Our Lord Immanuel.

As Fits the Holy Christmas Birth

WILLIAM MAKEPEACE THACKERAY

As fits the holy Christmas birth,
    Be this, good friends, our carol still—
Be peace on earth, be peace on earth,
    To men of gentle will.

Songs of Christmas

HELEN LOWRIE MARSHALL

What is there about Christmas songs
*   That makes us love them so?*
This year—last year—the year before—
*   A hundred years ago—*

Then, as now, hearts thrilled to hear
*   The grand old carols ring,*
As happy carolers proclaimed
*   The birthday of the King.*

Now, as then, the magic of
*   Each old familiar strain*
Brings to mind the beauty
*   Of the season once again.*

We see the "little town of Bethlehem"
*   In quiet lie,*
Asleep beneath the glory
*   Of that star high in the sky.*

We sense the calm and peaceful hush—
*   The gentle, radiant light*
That brought "joy to the world" upon
*   That "silent, holy night."*

And when the children sing
*   Of Santa Claus and jingle bells,*
What glorious hope and happiness
*   Their jolly music tells.*

What is there about Christmas songs
*   That makes us love them all?*
Perhaps it's partly all the lovely
*   Things that they recall.*

While Shepherds Watched Their Flocks by Night

NAHUM TATE

Nahum Tate, poet laureate to Queen Anne, was responsible for writing this simple, yet most direct Nativity hymn. It was published in 1696 in his *New Version of the Psalms of David*.

Based on the description of the Nativity in Luke 2:8–14, it has become a permanent part of our Christmas season. The music by George Frederick Handel comes from an aria in his opera *Siroe*, composed in 1728.

> While shepherds watched their flocks by night,
> All seated on the ground,
> The angel of the Lord came down,
> And glory shone around.
> "Fear not," said he, for mighty dread
> Had seized their troubled mind;
> "Glad tidings of great joy I bring
> To you and all mankind.
>
> "To you, in David's town, this day,
> Is born of David's line,
> The Savior, who is Christ the Lord;
> And this shall be the sign;
> The heavenly Babe you there shall find
> To human view displayed,
> All meanly wrapped in swathing bands,
> And in a manger laid."
>
> Thus spake the seraph, and forthwith
> Appeared a shining throng
> Of angels, praising God, who thus
> Addressed their joyful song:
> "All glory be to God on high,
> And to the earth be peace;
> Goodwill henceforth from heaven to men
> Begin, and never cease."

Once in Royal David's City

CECIL FRANCES ALEXANDER

This beautiful Christmas hymn was written by Mrs. Cecil Frances Alexander, wife of the primate of Ireland. She wrote many hymns and carols, among them being "There Is a Green Hill Far Away." This particular carol was believed to be written for her godchildren who were bored with their Bible lessons. The story is told so simply, yet is so deeply moving—especially the fifth verse which begins, "And our eyes at last shall see Him . . ."

The hymn was published in 1848, with the melody being composed by a nine-year-old boy named Henry J. Gauntlett, who was organist at his father's church in Olney, England. At age fifteen the congregation was amazed to hear him give a glorious performance of Handel's *Messiah.*

Once in royal David's city
Stood a lowly cattle-shed,
Where a mother laid her Baby
In a manger for His bed;
Mary was that mother mild,
Jesus Christ her little Child.

He came down to earth from heaven,
Who is God and Lord of all,
And his shelter was a stable
And His cradle was a stall;
With the poor, and mean, and lowly,
Lived on earth our Savior holy.

And our eyes at last shall see Him,
Through His own redeeming love;
For that Child so dear and gentle
Is our Lord in heav'n above;
And He leads His children on
To the place where He is gone.

Not in that poor lowly stable,
With the oxen standing by,

142

We shall see Him, but in heaven,
Set at God's right hand on high;
When like stars His children crowned,
All in white shall wait around.

God Rest You Merry, Gentlemen

This carol, full of Christian joy, is one of the most popular in England. It brings to our minds scenes of "Merrie Old England" and probably dates from the sixteenth century. The author is unknown. It was first published in 1846 and harmonized by Sir John Stainer in 1867.

Charles Dickens referred to it in his classic *A Christmas Carol* when a young caroler began to sing, "God bless you merry, gentleman," through Scrooge's keyhole. "Scrooge seized the ruler with such energy of action that the singer fled in terror, leaving the keyhole to the fog and even more congenial frost."

The word "rest" in the opening line is the Old English term meaning "keep."

God rest you merry, Gentlemen,
Let nothing you dismay,
For Jesus Christ our Savior
Was born on Christmas Day;
To save us all from Satan's pow'r,
When we were gone astray:
O tidings of comfort and joy.

Now to the Lord sing praises,
All you within this place,
And with true love and brotherhood
Each other now embrace;
This holy tide of Christmas
All others doth efface:
O tidings of comfort and joy.

O Holy Night

ADOLPHE ADAM

A story is told of the effect this beautiful, haunting French carol had during the Franco-Prussian War. French and German soldiers were facing each other in opposite trenches on Christmas Eve, 1870.

Suddenly, a young Frenchman leaped out of his trench and began singing Adolphe Adam's magnificent "Cantique de Noël" (O Holy Night). The Germans were awestruck and not a shot was fired. Then a German climbed out of his trench and sang Martin Luther's Christmas hymn, "From Heaven to Earth I Come."

Adolphe Adam was born in Paris in 1803. Years later, people flocked to the city at Christmastime to hear his popular composition performed in the prominent churches. Originally it was meant for the single voice and even today is one of the most well loved of all Christmas solos.

The original words were written by M. Cappeau de Roquemaure and translated by John S. Dwight.

O holy night! the stars are brightly shining,
It is the night of the dear Savior's birth!
Long lay the world in sin and error pining,
'Til He appear'd, and the soul felt its worth.
A thrill of hope, the weary world rejoices,
For yonder breaks a new and glorious morn!
Fall on your knees!
O hear the angel voices!
O night divine! O night when Christ was born!
O night divine! O night, O night divine!

Led by the light of Faith serenely beaming,
With glowing hearts by His cradle we stand.
So, led by light of a star sweetly gleaming,
Here came the wise men from the Orient land.
The King of Kings lay thus in lowly manger,
In all our trials born to be our friend;
He knows our need, to our weakness no stranger;
Behold your King!
Before the Lowly bend!
Behold your King! your King! before Him bend.

Truly He taught us to love one another;
His law is love, and His gospel is peace;
Chains shall He break, for the slave is our brother,
And in His name all oppression shall cease.
Sweet hymns of joy in grateful chorus raise we,
Let all within us praise His holy name;
Christ is the Lord,
Oh, praise His name forever!
His pow'r and glory evermore proclaim!
His pow'r and glory evermore proclaim!

Christmas

PHILLIPS BROOKS

The earth has grown old with its burden of care
  But at Christmas it always is young,
The heart of the jewel burns lustrous and fair
And its soul full of music breaks forth on the air,
  When the song of the angels is sung.

The feet of the humblest may walk in the field
  Where the feet of the holiest have trod,
This, this is the marvel to mortals revealed
When the silvery trumpets of Christmas have pealed,
  That mankind are the children of God.

O Come, All Ye Faithful

(*Adeste Fideles*)

JOHN FRANCIS WADE

An Englishman named John Francis Wade was responsible for bringing this worshipful hymn to us. He traveled throughout Europe copying music for Catholic institutions and families. In Douai, France, he wrote the words and music and included them in a manuscript he was working on at the time. In 1750 it had its first public performance when it was included in the services at the Roman Catholic University in Lisbon.

Thirty-five years later it was sent to the Portuguese Embassy in London and received the name "Portuguese Hymn," after being sung in their chapel. By the Catholics it was called "Adeste, Fideles" and by the Protestants, "O Come, All Ye Faithful," after being translated by Canon Frederick Oakley in 1852.

There has been a mystery clouding the authorship for many years but it is now believed to be the work of this traveling copyist, John Francis Wade.

The words are so compelling and triumphant as they call believers to worship our Lord.

> *O come, all ye faithful, joyful and triumphant,*
> *O come ye, O come ye to Bethlehem.*
> *Come and behold Him, born the King of angels;*
> *O come let us adore Him, Christ the Lord.*
>
> *Sing, choirs of angels, sing in exultation,*
> *Sing, all ye citizens of heaven above.*
> *Glory to God, all glory in the highest.*
> *O come let us adore Him, Christ the Lord.*
>
> *Yea, Lord, we greet thee, born this happy morning,*
> *Jesus, to thee be all glory given.*
> *Word of the Father, now in flesh appearing;*
> *O come let us adore Him, Christ the Lord.*

Sing a Song of Christmas Carols

MARJORIE HOLMES

Deck the Halls with Boughs of Holly . . . And wash the curtains and polish the silver. And clean out the fireplace and haul in the wood . . . And try to find the old tree base. And dig out those cartons of decorations to see how many are good for another year.

While Shepherds Watched Their Flocks by Night . . . Sit up late making doll clothes. And finishing a sweater and painting a sled. And helping your husband uncrate a bicycle . . . And then steal around checking on your own flock before collapsing into bed.

Good Christian Men, Rejoice . . . When the last box is finally wrapped and tied and in the mail, and you're at least halfway through addressing the greeting cards.

We Three Kings of Orient Are . . . Bearing gifts we traverse afar: to church and parties and school bazaars. And shut-ins and hospitals and children's homes. And that family whose mother is ill and whose father is out of a job.

O Come, All Ye Faithful . . . Joyful and triumphant that somehow it's all done! The church bells are ringing, it's time to come . . . Come, children and neighbors and aunts and uncles and cousins—come and behold Him, O come let us adore Him!

Away in a Manger . . . No crib for a bed—a three-year-old is curled up in a pew, fast asleep.

It Came Upon the Midnight Clear . . . That little voice calling out: "Is it morning yet? Did Santa Claus come?"

Silent Night, Holy Night . . . All is calm, all is bright . . . at last . . . It is, it truly is . . . Sleep in heavenly peace.

Hark! the Herald Angels Sing . . . At the crack of dawn, "Get up, get up. Merry Christmas!"

Joy to the World . . . Let earth receive her king . . . And people their gifts, and parents their hugs . . . Let children run back and forth to each other's houses, and neighbors pop in for a cup of wassail and to admire the shining tree . . . Let heaven and nature and your own heart sing!

God Rest You Merry, Gentlemen . . . And women. Let nothing you dismay! Even though the whole house is an explosion of candy, nuts, papers, presents and ribbons; the tags are so mixed up nobody knows who to thank for what; and the cat is knocking the ornaments off the tree.

Add another log to the fire snapping so fragrant on the grate, baste the turkey already golden in the oven. Fling open the door to grand-parents and other guests who come tramping up the snowy walk. With true love and brotherhood, each other now embrace.

God rest you merry, mothers and fathers and families and friends, at the end of this glorious Christmas Day!

We Three Kings of Orient Are

JOHN HENRY HOPKINS, JR.

This carol conjures up scenes of Christmas pageants, children with homemade crowns and robes, bearing gifts. It has always intrigued young people with the drama of the story. Actually it is a small master-piece with words and music written by John Henry Hopkins, Jr., in 1857, who was rector of Christ's Church, Williamsport, Pennsylvania.

It is one of the few carols based on the story of the Wise Men in Matthew 2:1–12. The tradition of there being only three Wise Men per-haps was derived from there being three gifts given to the Baby Jesus. The gifts are symbolic of Jesus Christ. Gold stands for Christ's royalty, frankincense for His divinity and myrrh for His suffering.

Through the years there has been established a legend that the Wise Men arrived twelve days after Jesus' birth. Through this developed the custom of Twelfth Night, when gifts are exchanged and the Christmas season comes to a close.

THE THREE KINGS: *We three kings of Orient are,*
Bearing gifts we traverse afar
Field and fountain, moor and mountain,
Following yonder star.

REFRAIN

O star of wonder, star of night,
Star with royal beauty bright,
Westward leading, still proceeding,
Guide us to thy perfect light.

MELCHIOR: *Born a King on Bethlehem's plain,*
Gold I bring to crown Him again;
King forever, ceasing never
Over us all to reign.

REFRAIN

CASPAR: *Frankincense to offer have I,*
Incense owns a Deity nigh;
Prayer and praising, all men raising,
Worship Him, God on high.

REFRAIN

BALTHAZAR: *Myrrh is mine; its bitter perfume*
Breathes a life of fathering gloom;
Sorrowing, sighing, bleeding, dying,
Sealed in the stone-cold tomb.

REFRAIN

ALL: *Glorious now behold Him arise,*
King, and God, and Sacrifice;
Heav'n sings Alleluia;
Alleluia the earth replies.

REFRAIN

149

Christmas

From *The Dean's Watch*

ELIZABETH GOUDGE

Every year, at half-past five on Christmas Eve, Michael lifted his great fist and struck the double quarter, and the Cathedral bells rang out. They pealed for half an hour and all over the city, and in all the villages to which the wind carried the sound of the bells, they knew that Christmas had begun. People in the fen wrapped cloaks about them and went out of doors and stood looking toward the city. This year it was bitterly cold but the wind had swept the clouds away and the Cathedral on its hill towered up among the stars, light shining from its windows. Below it the twinkling city lights were like clustering fireflies about its feet. The tremendous bells' music that was rocking the tower and pealing through the city was out here as lovely and far away as though it rang out from the stars themselves, and it caught at men's hearts. "Now 'tis Christmas," they said to each other, as their forebears had said for centuries past, looking toward the city on the hill and the great fane that was as much a part of their blood and bones as the fen itself. "'Tis Christmas," they said, and went back happy to their homes.

In the city, as soon as the bells started, everyone began to get ready. Then from nearly every house family parties came out and made their way up the steep streets toward the Cathedral. Quite small children were allowed to stay up for the carol service, and they chattered like sparrows as they stumped along buttoned into their thick coats, the boys gaitered and mufflered, the girls with muffs and fur bonnets. It was the custom in the city to put lighted candles in the windows on Christmas Eve and their light, and the light of the street lamps, made of the streets ladders of light leaning against the hill. The grown-ups found them Jacob's ladders tonight, easy to climb, for the bells and the children tugged them up.

Nearly everyone entered by the west door, for they loved the thrill of crossing the green under the moon and stars, and mounting the steps and gazing up at the west front, and then going in through the Porch of Angels beneath Michael and the pealing bells. Some of them only came to the Cathedral on this one day in the year, but as they entered the nave they felt the impact of its beauty no less keenly than those who came often. It was always like a blow between the eyes, but especially at night, and especially on Christmas Eve when they were full of awe and

150

expectation. There were lights in the nave but they could do no more than splash pools of gold here and there, they could not illumine the shadows above or the dim unlighted chantries and half-seen tombs. The great pillars soared into darkness and the aisles narrowed to twilight. Candles twinkled in the choir and the high altar with its flowers was ablaze with them, but all the myriad flames were no more than seed pearls embroidered on a dark cloak. The great rood was veiled in shadow. All things alike went out into mystery. The crowd of tiny human creatures flowed up the nave and onto the benches. The sound of their feet, of their whispering voices and rustling garments, was lost in the vastness. The music of the organ flowed over them and they were still.

Hallelujah!

From *The Messiah*

GEORGE FREDERICK HANDEL

The kingdom of this world is become
the kingdom of our Lord and of His Christ,
and He shall reign for ever and ever.
King of kings and Lord of lords.
        HALLELUJAH!

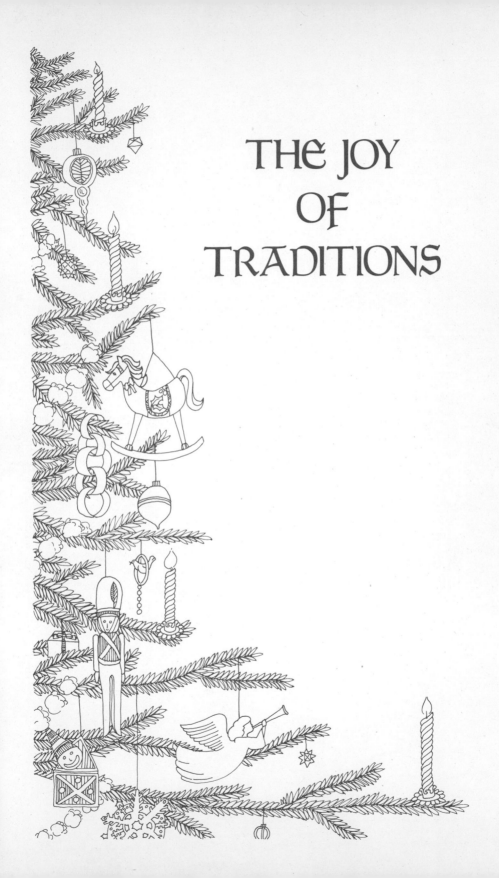

THE JOY
OF
TRADITIONS

Sing We All Merrily

Author unknown

Sing we all merrily
    Christmas is here,
The day that we love best
    Of days in the year.

Bring forth the holly,
    The box, and the bay,
Deck out our cottage
    For glad Christmas Day.

Sing we all merrily,
    Draw around the fire,
Sister and brother,
    Grandsire, and sire.

Making Your Christmas Merry

BILLY GRAHAM

When at this season of the year we wish our friends a "Merry Christmas," it is essential to realize that true merriment of heart is contingent upon the recognition of the truth that Christ was born in Bethlehem for our salvation. The word "merry" is from an old Anglo-Saxon word which sometimes meant "famous," "illustrious," "great," or "mighty." Originally, to be merry did not imply to be merely mirthful, but strong and gallant. It was in this sense that gallant soldiers were called "merry men." Favorable weather was called "merry weather." Brisk winds were called a "merry gale." Spenser speaks of London as "merry London." The word "merry" carries with it the double thought of "might" and "mirth," and is used both ways in Scripture. One of the early Christmas carols was "God Rest You Merry, Gentlemen." The Christian is to engage in spiritual merriment as he thinks upon the fact that, through the redemption, he becomes a child of God's family . . . The Bible teaches that the angels made merry at Christ's birth.

"Merry Christmas" in Many Languages

JOAN WINMILL BROWN

Argentina	Felices Pascuas
Armenia	Schenorhavor Dzenount
Belgium (Flemish)	Vrolijke Kerstmis
Brazil (Portuguese)	Boas Festas
Bulgaria	Chestita Koleda
China	Kung Hsi Hsin Nien or Bing Chu Shen Tan
Czechoslovakia	Vesele Vanoce
Denmark	Glaedelig Jul
Estonia	Roomsaid Joulu Puhi
Finland	Hauskaa Joulua
France	Joyeux Noël
Germany	Fröhliche Weihnachten
Greece	Kala Christougena
Holland	Zalig Kerstfeest
Hungary	Boldog Karacsony
Iraq	Idah Saidan Wa Sanah Jadidah
Ireland (Gaelic)	Nodlaig Nait Cugat
Italy	Buon Natale
Japan	Meri Kurisumasu
Mexico	Feliz Navidad
Norway	Gledelig Jul
Poland	Wesolych Swiat
Portugal	Boas Festas
Romania	Sarbatori Vesele
Russia	S Roshestvóm Khristóvym
South Africa (Afrikaans)	Een Plesierige Kerfees
Spain	Felices Pascuas
Sweden	Glad Jul
Turkey	Noeliniz Ve Yeni Yiliniz Kutlu Olsun
Ukraine	Chrystos Rozdzajetsia Slawyte Jeho
Wales	Nadolig Llawen
Yugoslavia (Croatian)	Srećan Božić
Yugoslavia (Serbian)	Hristos se rodi

The Promise of Christmas

HELEN STEINER RICE

Nothing I write the whole year through . . . Means more to me than this card to YOU . . . For you're more to me than a NAME and a FACE . . . More than SOME ONE I met SOME PLACE . . . You're one of Christ's messengers, sent to fulfill . . . His Christmas promise of PEACE and GOODWILL . . . For only through folks I have met, like you . . . Can the PROMISE of CHRISTMAS ever come true . . . For the feeling of friendship that stirs the heart . . . To send Christmas greetings is only the start . . . Of something deeper that's hidden inside . . . That we cover up with an "armor of pride" . . . But from time to time, it's bound to peek through . . . And I've glimpsed it often in folks like you . . . And that's why at Christmas I can never forgo . . . Sending a message to all those I know . . . For somehow I feel YOU and I are a PART . . . Not just of "each other" but Christ's own heart . . . And He came at Christmas so we might find . . . That it's not enough to be "casually kind" . . . For life can only be PEACEFUL and GOOD . . . When we are LOVED and UNDERSTOOD . . . And there's only one way to understand . . . And that's to follow Christ's "new command" . . . "LOVE YE ONE ANOTHER AS I LOVED YOU" . . . Not just as friends and acquaintances do . . . For Christmas is more than a merry greeting . . . Christ gave it to us as a "SPIRITUAL MEETING" . . . So, blessed be the CHRISTMAS TIE that binds . . . The love in our hearts to the thoughts in our minds . . . And to those I've just met and to those I have known . . . MERRY CHRISTMAS, GOD BLESS YOU and MAKE YOU HIS OWN.

The Importance of Traditions

EDITH SCHAEFFER

Our traditions connected with Christmas are very special. Our four children and their families have their own careful Christmas traditions—some are the same ones we had and some are different ones. For all of our twenty-eight years in Switzerland we have had the five o'clock Christmas Eve service in Champéry, with over a hundred candles to be put in wooden candleholders made of rough logs, and also fastened on fresh green trees. The supper at home has always started with cream of tomato soup with salted whipped cream on top, and has had a main course of easy-to-serve ham and potato chips and salad with special trimmings and homemade rolls. The apple-mince pies with crisscross crusts (or pumpkin if you would rather) are also a traditional dessert. The Christmas tree has been trimmed the night before, during a traditional time of drinking iced ginger ale and eating homemade Christmas cookies spread out in lovely rows on a tray. The Christmas stockings, filled with all sorts of interesting but inexpensive things, are the old hand-knitted stockings our girls wore the first years in Switzerland. Full of holes, but still usable, they add much in the way of memories as they are pulled out one night and filled and then found on Christmas morning. There are always tangerines to be eaten as we come to them, and homemade Christmas bread, along with tea or hot vanilla eggnog to be enjoyed in the bedroom as we open the stockings. The traditional lunch of homemade rolls (filled with thin beef), tomato juice, olives and pickles, and either milk shakes or ginger-ale floats for dessert is eaten whenever we feel hungry, sitting around the Christmas tree, opening gifts. There is the customary reading of Luke 2 and prayer together before eating. For dinner in the evening, there is a traditional tablecloth of lovely thin linen with appliquéd deer on it (bought at a sale in Philadelphia twenty years ago and used every Christmas since).

There is something about saying, "We *always* do this," which helps to keep the years together. Time is such an elusive thing that if we keep on meaning to do something interesting, but never do it, year would follow year with no special thoughtfulness being expressed in making gifts, surprises, charming table settings, and familiar, favorite food.

Christmas with the ten Booms

CORRIE TEN BOOM

❄

I am going to tell you how Betsie and I celebrated Christmas in Holland. We worked like a real team and often were the speakers at eight or ten Christmas feasts. In clubs, Sunday schools, hospitals, military groups, and churches—whenever we got a chance.

The Christmas treats were usually the same—Christmas bread with powdered sugar on it and raisins. There was an orange for every child, too. At that time there were no sweet ones in the whole of Holland, and I still remember the sour taste! But it was a joy—a special Christmas joy. Then a cup of hot cocoa. And whenever it was possible, a Christian booklet and a text for the wall with birdies and flowers around a Bible word.

Most of the time we arranged activities in this way: At the first feast Betsie told *the* Christmas story of Luke 2 and I told *a* Christmas story. At the second one we did the opposite—Betsie told *a* story and I *the* story.

In the watchmaking business it was very busy those Christmas days. I can remember that when we went to the feast, tired after a full day, I would count for myself, *"Number four.* Five more evenings—and then we are through Christmas!"

I knew that was wrong and I prayed: *Lord, give me the miracle that I won't get tired but enjoy every Christmas feast, even if it is number ten. Should it not mean joy for everyone that You were born in Bethlehem? So Betsie and I must feel joy to be Your channel.*

God answered that prayer, and all the years we did it, that miracle happened.

. . . Christmas was a feast in our Beje home. Mother and the aunts had a gift for making it as colorful and happy as possible. I remember the holly and the mistletoe—the Christmas table with the red ribbons. Sometimes even a little Christmas tree.

Tante Jans always gave her soldiers a Christmas book and the bookstore sent us a great number from which to choose the best ones. Even as a child I remember the joy of reading through and looking at all those books.

The climax of the feast in the Beje was when we were enjoying Christmas Eve with stories and the singing of carols.

Tante Jans could tell a story so beautifully that nobody could stop listening to her. I remember that the real Christmas event was clearly stressed by her and by Father, who read the Bible from a booklet where you could read not only Luke but also the other Gospels—Matthew 2 following Luke 2, verse 20. All the happenings then followed each other as one great story. Both Father and Tante Jans made it so clear to us that Christmas was for all of us. For *me*. Jesus came for *me*. Jesus was my friend, my Savior.

The Deeper Meaning of Christmas

MARY C. CROWLEY

Sometimes we tend to get lost in the traditional lore of the Christmas season—the Christmas tree, the visit from Santa Claus, and the feverish giving of gifts. Yet if we truly worship the Christ child in our hearts, we can make each tradition become a part of the deeper meaning of Christmas.

The Christmas tree will inevitably and properly suggest the one who grew to manhood to bear "our sins in his own body on the tree, that we might die to sin and live to righteousness" (1 Peter 2:24).

Family reunions will point to the truth that where two or three are gathered together, there Christ is, in the midst, as well as to the family of the Redeemed. The dinners and the parties will speak of the Christ who hallowed feasts when He walked this earth and who constitutes the "living bread which came down from heaven" (John 6:51).

The centrality of children at this blessed season should remind us that childlike faith before the mysteries of the Incarnation is a requisite for participation in His Kingdom.

Even Santa Claus, who comes from a land of snow-white purity to give gifts to those who have nothing of their own, proclaims to all who have ears to hear the message of the entrance of God into our sinful world to "give gifts to men."

Christmas thus calls for total appropriation and reconsecration. Human love and worship of Christ as we sing our heartwarming carols, as we trim our trees, and as we share our love with gifts—both given and received.

O Lord, may the deeper glory of Christmas invade our hearts and give a glow to our homes and families.

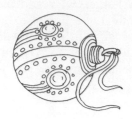

Tradition Time

HELEN LOWRIE MARSHALL

So much of the joy of Christmas
    Is the sameness of it all—
Always the wreath upon the door,
    The festoons in the hall;
The mistletoe hung overhead,
    The squeals at getting captured;
The sparkling tree that holds its viewers
    Silently enraptured.

The same beloved ornaments,
    The candles and the bells;
The same old Christmas stories
    That Grandpa always tells.
The same old battered angel
    Once again adds to the joy—
It's stood atop the tree each year
    Since Grandpa was a boy.

The merry family gatherings—
    The old, the very young;
The strangely lovely way they
    Harmonize in carols sung.
For Christmas is tradition time—
    Traditions that recall
The precious memories down the years,
    The sameness of them all.

Christmas at Our House

RUTH BELL GRAHAM AND
GIGI GRAHAM TCHIVIDJIAN

Do you ever have oysters for breakfast?

We do, once a year, on Christmas morning.

Perhaps you wonder why we have them then. When I go to the grocery store the day before Christmas and ask for oysters, I like to tell the man when I'm going to serve them.

"Oysters for breakfast!" he says, and he is very puzzled. Then I explain that my mother always served oyster stew for Christmas breakfast when I was a girl in China. It was a family custom. And when my father, who is a doctor, decided that it was time to bring his family back to America we brought back the custom of oysters for Christmas breakfast, too.

. . . Let's say that it's Christmas morning. The tree is over there by the window, with the presents beneath it and its branches loaded down with warm-colored lights, candy canes, ornaments, and the smallest gifts. And here in front of the enormous fireplace—big enough to stand up in, when there's no fire—are the stockings, one for every child and cousin . . . The presents have to wait until after breakfast, but the stockings are for now.

After the stockings comes breakfast, and you know what is on the table today, don't you? Oysters, floating in a big, steaming stew. (Want to know a secret? Personally, I don't like oysters for breakfast. I never did, not even when I was a girl back in China. But the stew part is fine.)

Our children think breakfast takes forever on Christmas morning. Never do the grown-ups eat so much. They sit around and drink cup after cup of coffee, and they lean back and talk about how long it's been since they were all together, and they even waste precious minutes looking out over the valley and saying what a lovely day it is. But then comes the wonderful moment when finally they're through, and they get up, scraping their chairs on the floor, and everyone goes back into the living room to open the presents.

It takes a long time because everyone wants to see what everyone else has received. But finally the very last package is opened. The floor is a heap of paper and ribbons and the grown-ups are saying, as they did last year, that there's really too much and that next year they will have to buy fewer presents.

And now comes the moment that's really Christmas. The fire is snapping. Christmas music is playing softly on the record player. Everyone makes himself comfortable, some on the floor, some in chairs, some on the window seat. It's time for the Christmas story. Father opens the Bible to the second chapter of the Book of Luke. When he begins to read the room is suddenly still with a special stillness that it has only at this time on Christmas morning. We are very quiet as we listen again to the wonderful story.

[Ruth and Billy Graham's five children are all grown now, with families of their own. The traditions they learned as children were many and are a cherished part of their lives.

Gigi, the Graham's eldest daughter, now married to Stephan Tchividjian, tells this delightful, honest and amusing story of her small son's reaction to the family traditions!]

Christmas arrived, with all the joy, excitement, and anticipation that usually accompanies this happy holiday. Our children had been making endless lists for weeks, and each time I was shown another one, I would reply automatically, "Wait until Christmas."

Finally, all was ready, wrapped, and packed for the trip to North Carolina. The closer we got to the mountains and grandparents, the more excited the voices in the car became. The first glimpse of "home," as we drove up the winding drive, and the warm welcome that awaited us—along with homemade apple pie and a cozy fire—all added to our excitement.

This excitement, and the anticipation of all that was yet to come, built to a crescendo on Christmas Eve, as each child (and adult) hung his or her stocking in front of the large fireplace. My daddy gathered all the children around and called Santa, at the North Pole—just to make sure he had received all the lists and everything was in order—then wished him a good and speedy trip. Just as the children were all being hurried off to bed, Santa's sleigh bells could be heard above the roof. (They were donkey's bells hung on the chimney and rung by my younger brother at the appropriate moment.) Needless to say, sleep didn't come easily to the children that night.

Christmas morning arrived, and everyone rushed down to the kitchen, dressed in their Sunday best. By tradition, no one is allowed into the living room until all have gathered and finished eating. The children tried to be patient, as the grown-ups slowly drank their coffee and munched their rolls. Just as the last drop of coffee was being downed, my daddy decided it would be better to read the Christmas story before the stockings, instead of later. Amid sighs, he began to read the beautiful story.

Even though the children listened, I am afraid they didn't hear much, that morning.

Then, to make matters worse, my sister decided pictures should be taken as each child entered the living room, so the children were told to line up and enter one by one. This did it. My eldest son looked up at his grandmother and said, in total disgust and exasperation, "Bethlehem was never as miserable as this!"

O Christmas Tree

TRADITIONAL GERMAN CAROL

O Christmas tree, O Christmas tree,
How lovely are your branches.
In summer sun, in winter snow,
A dress of green you always show.
O Christmas tree, O Christmas tree,
How lovely are your branches.

O Christmas tree, O Christmas tree,
With happiness we greet you.
When decked with candles once a year,
You fill our hearts with yuletide cheer.
O Christmas tree, O Christmas tree,
With happiness we greet you.

Joni's Miracle of Christmas

JOAN WINMILL BROWN

Family traditions had always added to the warmth and joy of Christmas for Joni Eareckson and her family. For her the season was always filled with excitement and anticipation.

That was until Christmas, 1967—five months after the swimming accident that left her a quadriplegic. No more could she run out in the snow to sing carols for the neighbors. It seemed all the pleasures of the season were gone forever. Joni and her family shed no tears, but the atmosphere at the Eareckson home was one of great sadness.

That year the traditions were the same; the decorations lovingly made from the holly and greenery which grew so profusely on their farm; the gathering of family and friends; a birthday cake baked especially for Jesus, which had become a treasured custom over the years together with the singing of "Happy Birthday, dear Jesus." In spite of all these familiar traditions Joni felt she would never again experience the joy of Christmas.

Over the years since her accident, Joni has learned to accept her handicap without resentment or bitterness. Her change of attitude has become a glorious tribute to the grace of God. Today, about Christmas, she says:

"Does Christmas excite you? It sure does me and I love every minute of it. The taste of hot apple cider, the smell of fresh fragrant pines, the carols, the worship and adoration of Jesus."

Joni has developed her remarkable talent for painting by holding a brush between her teeth. Slowly and laboriously, brush mark by brush mark, she has mastered the art of bringing imaginative life to a canvas. Among many beautiful paintings, Joni has executed a tender and inspiring rendering of "The Annunciation." About that painting she recalls:

"As I sat back and took a long look at the completed picture, I could not help but wonder at this miraculous mystery. God in the flesh, Christ incarnate, a divine baby. It is such an astounding miracle that it makes the rest of the miracles in the New Testament almost secondary. As we take the Incarnation by faith, so in turn the changing of water into wine, opening blind eyes to see, or even the raising of men from the dead seem no great matter for Jesus, the Incarnate. The miracle of His birth makes all the other miracles 'simple.'"

Up at the Top

HANS CHRISTIAN ANDERSEN

*. . . And up at the top was
fixed a large star of gold
tinsel; it was magnificent
beyond words!*

The Royal Christmas Tree

The Illustrated London News, *1848*

The Christmas tree is annually prepared by Her Majesty's command for the royal children . . . The tree employed for this festive purpose is a young fir of about eight feet high, and has six tiers of branches. On each tier, or branch, are arranged a dozen wax tapers. Pendant from the branches are elegant trays, baskets, bonbonnières, and other receptacles for sweetmeats of the most varied and expensive kind; and of all forms, colors, and degrees of beauty. Fancy cakes, gilt gingerbread and eggs filled with sweetmeats are also suspended by variously colored ribbons from the branches. The tree, which stands upon a table covered with white damask, is supported at the root by piles of sweets of a larger kind, and by toys and dolls of all descriptions, suited to the youthful fancy . . . On the summit of the tree stands the small figure of an angel, with outstretched wings, holding in each hand a wreath.

A Christmas Tree

From *Christmas Stories*

CHARLES DICKENS

I have been looking on, this evening, at a merry company of children assembled round that pretty German toy, a Christmas tree. The tree was planted in the middle of a great round table, and towered high above their heads. It was brilliantly lighted by a multitude of little tapers; and everywhere sparkled and glittered with bright objects. There were rosy-cheeked dolls, hiding behind the green leaves; there were real watches (with movable hands, at least, and an endless capacity of being wound up) dangling from innumerable twigs; there were French-polished tables, chairs, bedsteads, wardrobes, eight-day clocks, and various other articles of domestic furniture (wonderfully made, in tin, at Wolverhampton), perched among the boughs, as if in preparation for some fairy housekeeping; there were jolly, broad-faced little men, much more agreeable in appearance than many real men—and no wonder, for their heads took off, and showed them to be full of sugarplums; there were fiddles and drums; there were tambourines, books, workboxes, paint boxes, sweetmeat boxes, peep-show boxes, and all kinds of boxes; there were trinkets for the elder girls, far brighter than any grown-up gold and jewels . . . there were guns, swords and banners . . . pen wipers, smelling bottles . . . real fruit . . . imitation apples, pears and walnuts, crammed with surprises; in short, as a pretty child, before me, delightedly whispered to another pretty child, "There was everything, and more."

The Christmas Pine Tree

BORIS PASTERNAK

I love her to tears, at sight, from the first,
As she comes from the woods—
  in storm and snow.
So awkward her branches, the shyest of firs!
We fashion her threads unhurriedly, slow.
Her garments of silvery gossamer lace,
Patterns of tinsel, and spangles aglow
From branch unto branch down to the base.

From "*A Day of Pleasant Bread*"

DAVID GRAYSON

They have all gone now, and the house is very still. For the first time this evening I can hear the familiar sound of the December wind blustering about the house, complaining at closed doorways, asking questions at the shutters; but here in my room, under the green reading lamp, it is warm and still. Although Harriet has closed the doors, covered the coals in the fireplace, and said good-night, the atmosphere still seems to tingle with the electricity of genial humanity.

The parting voice of the Scotch preacher still booms in my ears:

"This," said he, as he was going out of our door, wrapped like an Arctic highlander in cloaks and tippets, "has been a day of pleasant bread."

One of the very pleasantest I can remember!

I sometimes think we expect too much of Christmas Day. We try to crowd into it the long arrears of kindliness and humanity of the whole year. As for me, I like to take my Christmas a little at a time, all through the year. And thus I drift along into the holidays—let them overtake me unexpectedly—waking up some fine morning and suddenly saying to myself:

"Why, this is Christmas Day!"

As We Leave Bethlehem

CHARLES L. ALLEN AND CHARLES WALLIS

Christmas has come and gone. Soon the decorations will be carefully packed away until another year. The elusive pine needles will be swept up. The children will be sent back to school. The thank-you notes will be written and the warm and glowing experience will become a memory.

Some people are also likely to put into a deep freezer their cheerfulness and goodwill. The boss will become as cranky as ever. People will become themselves once more. But it was good to see what a change could be wrought in the minds and hearts of men, even for a day! Yet Christmas need not be limited to only a day. Christmas can become, as it was meant to be, an attitude toward life that will continue during all of the days that follow.

The roads to Bethlehem were roads of hope and trust, of faith and charitableness. Bethlehem is not a dead end; it is rather the place from which we move with greater goodwill, deeper faith, more permanent peace of mind and heart. Joseph Fort Newton wrote:

> Christmas is a prophetic day, looking not so much backward as forward. It belongs to an order of life not yet attained, to a religion not yet realized; to a coming, but distant, time which all prophets have foreseen, when men will be ruled by "the angels of our higher nature," and justice will reign, and pity and joy will walk the common ways of life.

The Bible tells us not only of those who went to Bethlehem, but also of those who went away. The shepherds were watching their sheep on the hills round about Bethlehem when in a vision splendid they were told of Christ's birth. They hastened to His manger. Then they returned to their flocks, ". . . glorifying and praising God for all . . . they had heard and seen . . ." (Luke 2:20). Their rejoicing could not be extinguished with the coming of sunrise on the day after Christmas. Their joy was eternal. Around their campfires they rehearsed again and again the experiences until, I am sure, their lives, their homes, their work radiated with a continuing joyfulness.

The wise men had stopped at Herod's palace on their journey to Bethlehem. He asked them to visit him before they returned, but ". . . being warned . . . in a dream . . . not [to] return to Herod, they departed into their own country another way" (Matthew 2:12). And they returned by a different spiritual way; the old way of life was no longer satisfying. They had found in Bethlehem a new and a better way to live.

As we leave Bethlehem, we ought to leave behind old grudges, old fears, old sorrows. We ought to continue our adventure of life praising God and by walking on new and better roads. Sometime during the winter we shall need the friendly spirit of Christmas. Sometime in the spring we shall want the hope of Christmas. Let us not pack up the true spirit of Christmas when we put away the decorations.

So Remember

Author unknown

So remember while December
Brings the only Christmas Day,
In the year let there be Christmas
In the things you do and say;
Wouldn't life be worth the living
Wouldn't dreams be coming true
If we kept the Christmas spirit
All the whole year through?

171

Scrooge

From *A Christmas Carol*

CHARLES DICKENS

"I will honor Christmas in my heart, and try to keep it all the year."

For Christmas the Year Round

PETER MARSHALL

"O come to my heart, Lord Jesus:
There is room in my heart for Thee."

Lord Jesus, we thank Thee for the spirit shed abroad in human hearts at Christmas. Even as we invited Thee at Christmas to be born again in our hearts, so wilt Thou now go with us throughout the days ahead, to be our Companion in all that we do. Wilt Thou help each one of us to keep Christmas alive in our hearts and in our homes, that it may continue to glow, to shed its warmth, to speak its message during all the bleak days of winter.

May we hold to that spirit, that we may be as gentle and as kindly today as we were on Christmas Eve, as generous tomorrow as we were on Christmas morning.

Then if—by Thy help—we should live through a whole week in that spirit, it may be we can go into another week, and thus be encouraged and gladdened by the discovery that Christmas can last the year round.

So give us joyful, cheerful hearts to the glory of Jesus Christ, Lord, Amen.